Sunset on the Pacific:

Retirement Adventures In Nicaragua

By Jean B~~~~~~

Thank yo

interest + support

Jean

D0880299

ISBN: 978-0-9634203-1-2

Humans Anonymous Press
PO Box 18166
Asheville NC 28814

Photo credits:
Cover photo by Dan Polley
Photos by Jean Brugger except:
Photos on pages 9, 39, 60, 75, 79, 84, 107, 115,
and 145 by Cesar Paniamogen
Photo on page 34 by Diane Foertsch
Photos on pages 32, 117, 131, and rear cover
by Katie Brugger
Chapter heading photo by Dan Polley
Printed and bound in Canada by Art Bookbindery

Dedicated

to

Sister Maggie Fisher

Introduction

I had never intended to write a book, but after telling my story to many people, several suggested I should write it down so that friends and family would have a record of my adventures. This book is my attempt to share with you my Central American journey.

Perhaps I should begin with a little background, which, I'm sure you will agree, makes me an unlikely candidate for such a precipitous decision. I grew up in Canada and moved with my parents to the United States when I was a teenager. After graduating from high school, I attended nursing school and subsequently married a young doctor. It was the time of the Korean War and since Tom was subject to the draft, we were posted to Japan for two years. We were lucky because most doctors were sent straight to Korea where I would not have been able to join him. We were one of the few couples that ventured off the army base to mix with the local people. Most of our fellow Americans were happy staying on base where things were familiar and all their needs were met either in the PX or Commissary. This was my first experience in a foreign country with a different language and culture and perhaps set the stage for my future adventurousness.

I was a full-time housewife and mother, raising five children, the last few years on my own as Tom and I were divorced in 1975. At the time, the divorce seemed to be the end of my life as I knew it. Out of necessity I returned to work outside the home, and new horizons were opened to me that I would never have otherwise experienced. I had always been active in a church, but now I had the opportunity to develop a whole new circle of friends.

During the 1980s I began to take more of an interest in the policies of our government vis-à-vis other countries, particularly Central America. Why Central America? First of all, Central America was often the focus of President Reagan's anti-communism rhetoric so was frequently in the news. More importantly, I had begun to question the veracity of that rhetoric. My generation had been taught to believe that our leaders were honorable people who would never mislead or lie to their constituents.

As I read more extensively, particularly in alternative publications, and talked with others, including my own daughter Katie, I began to realize that what the young people of the '60s were saying was good advice: question rather than just accept what our leaders were proclaiming.

At a commemorative service honoring the memory of Oscar Romero, the Salvadoran martyr, I met a group of like-minded individuals who were members of an organization called Interfaith Coalition on Latin America which was directed by Sister Maggie Fisher. As I learned more and more about the wars our government was supporting there, primarily in Nicaragua and El Salvador, I began to take a more active part in the various activities sponsored by this group. In the early 1990s I made two trips to El Salvador.

The first took place while the war was still going on, so things were a little tense. We were told that if we were out walking and saw the local people drop to the ground, we should do likewise. As American citizens we didn't expect trouble and were fortunate that we had none but there were a few anxious moments when we were stopped by the military to have our documents checked. Our purpose was to visit women's groups and I was very impressed with their courage and strength in the face of so many threats and so much killing. I felt that I had much to learn from them.

My second visit was to monitor the election after the peace agreement had been signed. Sister Maggie accompanied the group and as we worked together we began a friendship that has lasted to this day. I didn't speak Spanish but we were told that we were only to observe and if we saw any irregularities we should notify the UN representative, rather than do anything ourselves. The people lined up in the hot sun all day to vote and we were present when they counted the votes that night by flashlight. It was exciting to be part of their first democratic vote.

As a result of those experiences, I decided to spend some time in Central America when I retired from my position as Parish Nurse Coordinator at Deaconess Health Services in St. Louis, Missouri.

Sister Maggie retired at about the same time as I did and had planned for some time to go to Nicaragua for two years to teach English. She allowed me to tag along. Many people questioned my decision since in the view of the U.S. State Department, which had instigated a civil war in the 1980s, Nicaragua was considered a dangerous place for an American to be. Not so!

We arrived in Nicaragua at the end of 1995 and took up residence in a guest house in Managua run by a retired Episcopal priest, Grant Gallup. I had no clear vision of what I would do in Nicaragua, but was sure I wanted to find a way to reach out to the people in some helping capacity. In the quest for my role, trying various options, I came to the conclusion that Nicaraguans were not only warm and welcoming but were very capable people, who just needed help to open up educational and job opportunities to improve their lives.

Nicaragua is a small Central American country situated between Honduras on the north and Costa Rica on the south. The east and west boundaries are the Caribbean Sea and the Pacific respectively. It is known as the land of lakes and volcanoes and for good reason. A line of volcanoes, some still active, runs from northwest to southeast across the country, and there are two very large lakes.

Nicaragua is thought to be the youngest part of the Central American isthmus, created by volcanic activity that closed the gap between North and South America. The lakes are the remnants of that activity and there is much speculation about the sharks that got caught in the larger of these lakes and adapted to fresh water. It also played a historic role at the time of the gold rush when many speculators found crossing through Nicaragua to be the quickest way to reach the west coast from the east coast of the U.S. When a canal was proposed to allow ships to cross the isthmus, Nicaragua was a major contender, but for political reasons Panama was chosen.

In February of 1996, Grant, Maggie, and I made a week-end trip to San Juan del Sur, a small fishing village on the Pacific coast of Nicaragua. I fell in love with this picturesque place and its people. That trip changed my life.

This then is my story.

1

When Maggie, Grant, and I made that first fateful trip to San Juan del Sur and I felt so drawn to this village, I persuaded Maggie that we should spend a month enjoying the beauty, the people, and the quietness that was so different from Managua. May was supposed to be a hot, dry, dusty time in Managua just prior to the rainy season, so it seemed like a good time to be elsewhere. Our challenge was to find a place where we could comfortably stay that was relatively close to the beach. We spent some time investigating options without finding a place we could agree on. Both Maggie and I were accustomed to living alone most of the time, so we knew we had to find a place where we could each have some privacy. We were directed to contact Chris Berry, a resident of San Juan, who could probably help us.

Chris is a North American who chose to leave his law practice in San Francisco in 1989 and sail around South America. He was feeling incredible stress from his work and also had some health problems so felt time away would be therapeutic. Chris had sailed twice around the world with his father so was very capable of piloting a sailboat on a prolonged journey. After three months sailing leisurely down the California and Central American coasts, he and a friend arrived in the bay of San Juan. Like me, they fell in love with this place and decided to stay. They lived on the boat and began to become involved in the community, studying Spanish, working with health brigades serving the isolated *campesinos*, teaching English, and facilitating the work of various mission groups by finding lodging and arranging for translators, among other things. However it finally became clear that they needed to find some way to support themselves. The boat seemed an ideal solution, so they began providing day-long cruises in the sailboat down the Pacific coast and back.

When Maggie and I met Chris his business had grown and he had trained a group of local young people to assist him. His friend had returned to the States due to family responsibilities. Chris was now renting a house in town. Living with him was a long-time friend from California, Leslie Sullivan, who had come to recuperate in San Juan after a chronic illness. Chris was quite willing to help us find lodging and took us to meet a family here in San Juan that rented out their house whenever it was possible, as it provided extra income. They would move in with relatives who lived right next door. It was a comfortable little house with a bedroom for each of us so we agreed on a price and the time frame, all this being facilitated by Chris. We left San Juan with the very pleasant prospect of returning for a month in May.

San Juan del Sur

During our month in San Juan, Chris continued to be very helpful to us. He suggested that we hire someone to assist us with household chores, but being two women used to that kind of work, we declined. It wasn't long until we were knocking at his door asking him to find us someone. We had forgotten that washing sheets and towels is not an easy task when there is no washing machine, and mopping floors like the Nicaraguan women do with such ease was, for us, an impossible task. Maggie, who had chosen to do that part of the household work left big swirls of mop marks all over the floor and neither of us could figure out how to erase them. Our helper cleared them up in minutes. I think Nicaraguans are born with a mop in their hands!

We did do our own personal laundry and cooking. It was fun to plan a menu for the day, then go to the local market for supplies. My job was the cooking and we ate a lot of fresh fish, vegetables, and fruit. Maggie had only agreed to come if we used part of the time for reflection so each morning we would share something we were reading followed by discussion of how it related to our individual lives. It enriched our time together immeasurably. Almost every evening we walked to the beach to enjoy a drink and a snack, while we watched the magnificent sunsets over the Pacific. I remember one in particular that filled the whole sky with color.

As Chris and Leslie were almost the only gringos in town besides us, we began to spend time together over an occasional dinner in the evening. We also decided to try out Chris' boat cruise. We enjoyed it so much that we went twice. The crew on the boat had been well trained by Chris and were so attentive that we felt very pampered.

Our last day in San Juan we walked to the other side of the bay to have lunch at a small restaurant called Lago Azul. It had been raining and on the way back, a little kitten walked out of the weeds at the side of the road. It was wet and cold so I asked Maggie for her kerchief to wrap it in. Maggie was less than enthusiastic as cats are not her favorite thing, but after I promised to wash it and return it to her clean, she agreed. We delivered the kitten to Chris' door knowing his love for cats (he had several) but at first he was reluctant to take in another. However, he soon relented saying that the bills for food and shelter would come to me each month. That cat is now one of the elders among our cat population.

As we got to know Chris better, he began to talk about his dream of building a small hotel in San Juan. He was weary of doing boat cruises and both he and the boat were growing older. He could also see the potential for tourism in San Juan del Sur and felt it was the right time to begin to build accommodations for future visitors. With Leslie's help, he had put together a business plan. All he was lacking was financial backing. As I reviewed his business plan, it occurred to me that this idea just might be the vehicle to actualize my wish to provide jobs and education for the young people of San Juan.

Maggie and I had many discussions about the implications and she was very helpful in looking at the pros and cons. I didn't have a lot of money but I did own my house in St. Louis, which I was willing to sell. By the end of the month we had begun to talk seriously about forming a partnership to realize our dreams.

After we returned to Managua and had some time to think things through, Maggie and I talked it over with Grant, our landlord, who had lived in Nicaragua since 1989. He was a little skeptical of the plan and urged caution. My youngest daughter, Diane, was coming for a two week visit so we agreed that during that time we would make a short visit to San Juan, where she could meet Chris, see the town and look at some property that Chris had in mind to buy. This was a fairly large piece of land, undeveloped, with lots of trees, a hilly terrain, and a small beach on the Pacific. Unfortunately it was difficult to access. However, we could see the potential and were already planning lodges, cabins, hiking trails, etc. Diane left with a very favorable impression of Chris, San Juan, and Nicaragua – both its beauty and its people. Her agreement that the idea was valid helped me make up my mind to go ahead.

Jean and Chris

Originally, I had planned to stay in Nicaragua for a year, after which I would return to the States to resume my "normal" life. I wasn't excited about the idea because on a trip the previous summer with my friend, Alice Peterson, I had come to the conclusion that I no longer wanted to live in a big city. Since I was retired and wasn't required to live in a place close to work, I decided that a small, beautiful place was where I wanted to be. I still had friends and one daughter living in St. Louis, but neither of those reasons was enough to keep me there even though my daughter relied on me for help in a variety of ways. Since she, like all my children was an adult, and my daughter, Katie, and her husband had encouraged me to do what I wanted to do rather than what I had done for years – put my children's needs first – I allowed myself to consider my own wishes for how I wanted to spend the balance of my life. The contemplation of a retirement community was an anathema to me. I felt I would be very unhappy living in an environment that included solely people my own age.

I finally decided that I wanted to help make this hotel project happen and fulfill my goals for helping the local people at the same time, so Chris and Leslie came to Managua to work out the details. My part was to provide the start-up funds and Chris and Leslie would provide the "sweat equity." Since I had to sell my house to acquire these funds, it meant that I would be living in Nicaragua, away from friends and family for the foreseeable future. This was more of a worry for Chris and Leslie than it was for me, at least at the time. I think the excitement of setting out on a new path overshadowed other considerations.

However the full impact had not sunk in. It was only after making the move that from time to time when I was walking on the beach, I would wonder what I was doing in another country, another culture, and having to learn a new language. Had I made a mistake? Was this really what I wanted to do? It was a little scary but exciting at the same time.

Another part of our agreement was that my immediate family could stay at the hotel at no cost, but of course, that wouldn't happen until some time in the future when we had a hotel to stay in. After spending six months in Nicaragua, I returned to the States to put my house on the market.

2

I arrived at my son Ron's house in Irvine, California at the end of June. It was good timing because the 6th of July was his 40th birthday and a big celebration was planned. My other son John and his wife would be attending. He and his family live in Vista, a town close to San Diego in southern California, about an hour's drive from Irvine.

It felt very strange to be back in the United States, the land of overwhelming abundance. I had not been in a supermarket for six months. I found the choices and variety almost more than I could handle. John and his family invited me to go with them to Disneyland a week or so later. Again I was overwhelmed by the assault on all my senses, while they took it all in stride. I stayed in California rotating between their homes until the end of July. The boys were very supportive of my plans, saying it was my life and my decision. That support helped me feel like what

I was doing was okay and that I wasn't crazy like some of my friends and relatives seemed to think.

When I had originally contemplated being in Nicaragua for a year I had leased my house to a friend for the time I would be gone. I fully expected that I would return to live in my house after the year was up. She had her own furnishings and wanted to use them so I had to decide what to do with my furniture. The smaller items could be stored in the basement as she was only planning to use it for laundry, but something needed to be done with the larger pieces.

I had two friends who were setting up transitional housing for abused women. These were women who had been in a shelter, but as there is a limit to the amount of time a woman can stay there, and many are not ready to resume their former lives, they needed a longer period of safety from their abuser. I admired them for what they were doing and offered my furniture to help furnish their first residence. They were delighted and accepted it with the provision that if I wanted the furniture when I returned they would be glad to give it back. With the help of church groups, among others, they have since gone on to establish several more residences in and around St. Louis. Many women from their program have been able to complete their high school education, find jobs, and make a comfortable home for themselves and their children.

Since my house was leased for a year and not available, I was homeless. My friend Alice Peterson asked me to live with her, at least during the interim. Alice and I had met in St. Louis in 1990 when she came from her home in St. Paul, Minnesota, to do volunteer work at the Deaconess Health System. We began a long friendship that ended only with her death in 2003.

While I waited for my house to sell, I lived in her home in St. Paul sporadically for a year and a half and we made several trips together including a camping trip to Alaska. We were almost always the oldest people in the campground so were quite a novelty. Alice's only requirement was that our campsite be near the bathroom, as she invariably needed to get up at night, and that it have flush toilets. One night we were staying in Jasper National Park in Alberta, Canada, and we knew there were black bears in the area, so I volunteered to accompany Alice if she was afraid to go alone to the bathroom. I must admit that I was a bit nervous and was relieved when she said no. Fortunately she didn't have a problem.

The ground was pretty hard on occasions and when it rained we invariably got wet and Alice got grumpy, but we thoroughly enjoyed our trip. One of the highlights was a trip on the inland ferry that delivers people and supplies to all the small towns along the British Columbia and Alaska coasts. Since we were in port at each stop for at least an hour, we were free to get off and walk around these small towns and admire some of the indigenous relics such as totem poles. During that trip we saw our first whales in the wild.

In the fall of 1996 I made a trip to St. Louis to visit my daughter and to put my house on the market. I was worried that I might have trouble selling it because it was in an area that had been threatened for years with the widening of highway 40, one of the main arteries in and out of St. Louis. My real estate agent assured me that the fact that it was an affordable house in the best school district in the St. Louis area would count more with prospective buyers than the possibility of losing it to highway improvement in the near future. The required city inspection indicated that some minor repairs had to be done before it could be put on the market and we needed to have the permission of the leasee to be able to show it while she was still living there. She willingly agreed.

While I was waiting for action on the house I decided to approach some others to see if they would like to invest in our project. Alice had already committed, so I turned to people I had met in Managua, thinking that they might be interested. Sandra George and John Detwyler, a couple who I had met at Grant's in Managua, expressed their willingness to participate. Chris had already made an offer on the property we liked and we were all intrigued with the idea of owning land on the Pacific coast. However, our hopes were dashed when Chris called to say our offer had been declined. Nothing had led us to believe that this could happen so we were very disappointed when we heard the news. I felt that this was an indication that it was not meant to be and had resigned myself to the possibility of taking my house off the market and returning to St. Louis.

However, Chris was not to be so easily deterred, which was a pattern frequently repeated in the years ahead. He had come across another piece of land that he was excited about. It was located on a hill overlooking the town and the ocean and he felt it an ideal spot for a hotel – close enough to town to visit and shop, yet separated enough to avoid all the traffic and other busyness of the town. I was a bit skeptical, having never seen this property, but Chris persuaded my friend Maggie, who was still living in Managua, to take a look at it. She was impressed. Relying on her good judgment, I agreed Chris should make an offer. Sandra and John helped make the down payment; the offer was made and accepted. We were on our way!

I thought that once I moved to Nicaragua I might not have the opportunity to see my brothers again, so I decided to visit them and share my plans with them. They were less than enthusiastic. They felt I was going to a dangerous place and, of most concern to my younger brother Don, that I was squandering my hard-earned money. Some of my friends felt the same way, but many, including my own children, admired me for my sense of adventure, especially at my age. My children's support was more important to me than what others might think.

During this time my tenant moved out of the house and some additional improvements were necessary to make it more attractive to buyers. I also had to decide what to do with my remaining belongings that were stored in the basement. Some larger items I sent to my sons in California and the smaller items to my daughters out of town. Mary, my daughter who lives in St. Louis, agreed to store the items I planned to take with me or just was not ready to give away. I also worked on my application for residency in Nicaragua, which was somewhat complicated given that we had no Nicaraguan embassy either in St. Paul or St. Louis. It had to be done by mail. Doing things electronically was not common then. I also began to think about how I was going to make the move with all the things I wanted to take. According to the residency information I was allowed to bring in a vehicle valued at $10,000 and a like amount in household goods. How was I going to do it?

After many unacceptable offers on the house, we finally got one in October, 1997 almost meeting our asking price. Closing was to be mid-December. I could begin planning for my trip. I had also heard from Chris that my Nicaraguan residency had been approved. Things finally seemed to be falling into place. It seemed that it was really going to happen. Still, I couldn't help but feel a little nervous about my decision. Was I being foolish as so many thought?

My task now was to decide how and when I was going to go. Chris had put me in touch with a friend of his from California, Bill Burtch. Bill had driven to Nicaragua many times and knew the ropes very well. He also spoke passable Spanish which was better than what I could do, even after studying for three weeks when I was in Nicaragua the first time.

If we were going to drive, I needed to buy a vehicle. I finally settled on a 1990 Mitsubishi Montero with 4-wheel drive. I sought the counsel of my son, Ron, who is very knowledgeable about cars, and of a local mechanic that my friend, Carolyn, recommended. The consensus was that it was a strong, tough vehicle, high enough to travel over the rough roads in Nicaragua. Bill and I agreed to meet mid-January in McAllen, Texas, and caravan from there. Since we would need to communicate while we were driving Bill had suggested by email that I stop at a pawn shop and buy a CB radio. I had never been in a pawn shop before so another new experience awaited me. My next task was choosing what I wanted to take and packing it all in the car. My daughter, Mary and Colin, her boyfriend, helped me organize and fit everything in.

On January 16th 1998, I left St. Louis, bound for McAllen and the beginning of a new life, different than I had ever known.

3

As I drove through Texas on my way to McAllen I came across a pawn shop and decided to check out their CB radios. Bill had told me I should be able to pick one up for $35-$40. I entered and a salesman asked me what I was looking for. When I explained what I wanted, he showed me some CBs but they seemed to be in a state of disrepair so I asked if there were any others. He went behind the counter and came up with a new hand-held CB. He said they were asking $65. I didn't know the protocol in pawn shops, but I innocently said, "My friend said I should pay no more than $35-$40." Immediately the salesman asked, "Well, how much are you willing to pay for this one?" I replied, "$40." He said he would have to check with the boss, but soon returned and said we had a deal. So much for my one and only experience in a pawn shop! I was proud of myself for managing to strike what I thought was a good deal my first time. Was it really? Who knows!

Bill was waiting at the motel in McAllen when I arrived and we hit it off right away. However, my room left a lot to be desired. The ceiling in one place was falling down and the bathroom was not clean. I had decided to find another motel, but Bill suggested I move in with him if I could stand his snoring. I did and we roomed together for the rest of the trip.

The next morning we were ready to set out, but thinking we would need a visa to enter Mexico with two cars, we decided to check with the Mexican Embassy. Sadly we discovered it was Martin Luther King Day and the Embassy was closed. Needless to say we were very disappointed. We certainly did not want to spend another night in McAllen. However, we were able to get some help from an official of the U.S. Consulate who provided us with the required visa, and at last we were on our way.

We crossed the border into Mexico without too much difficulty, but of course had delays. I had my first funny experience when a young man appeared at my window and asked for something which I presumed to be money. A friend in St. Louis had told me they were usually asking for a Coke so I handed him one. He gave me this very strange look but took it anyway. We drove with Bill in the lead until about 6:30 PM and then found a very nice motel in Almada, Mexico. Our agreement was to not drive after dark and if one of us needed to stop, to call the other on the radio.

The next day we drove down the east coast of Mexico. As we approached the Gulf of Mexico, the scenery became very beautiful. I was sorry that I had to pay such close attention to driving and couldn't look around much. The toll roads were excellent but the secondary roads were very bad. Most of the local people who had cars could not afford to pay the toll for the good road so they were used by truckers and people like ourselves. We by-passed Vera Cruz and stayed the night in a very nice hotel in a small town. Thankfully, Bill had travelled the route many times and knew clean, comfortable accommodations wherever we stayed. The next day we crossed from the Gulf side to the Pacific coast and again encountered beautiful scenery, very green and mountainous.

We were anxious to cross into Guatemala that day and heard that the border closed at 8 PM so decided we would try to do it. Unfortunately it was mass confusion at the border, and it took us several hours to cross. Our hotel was about 40 miles from the border and we drove the last couple of hours in the dark – not what we had planned – and then Bill made a wrong turn making us even later. I was a bit nervous because not too long before our trip a bus with young people from the U.S. had been stopped and robbed. I asked Bill what to do if someone jumped out in front of the car and he said, "If he is wearing a uniform, stop, otherwise keep on going." Fortunately we had no problems.

The next day we set out for El Salvador. We filled up with gas and the attendant managed to put 85 liters in my car even though the tank is only supposed to hold 75! The traffic going into Guatemala City was horrendous. Much of it was huge trucks carrying sugar cane. Fortunately we were able to take a by-pass, and I was grateful to leave all that traffic behind. For the most part the roads were good. As we approached El Salvador the scenery became very green with huge trees and mountains. It took us about four hours at the border into El Salvador, but other than waiting, we had no problems.

In Central America as you approach a border people come rushing up to your car hoping that you will hire them to help you with the paperwork required. It's a bit intimidating to see them surrounding your car and trying to outshout one another. You can do the paperwork yourself but it is very complicated so I left it to Bill to hire someone to help us. Some were people he had used before and they recognized him. However, I don't think it helped any with the price! We didn't have much trouble with the things we were carrying. We had prepared lists and they were accepted without a problem. Of course the list had to be in Spanish, and I was carrying my hammered dulcimer. That created a lot of confusion as "*dulce*" means "sweet" in Spanish.

Driving through El Salvador we encountered a lot of road construction and the tunnels through the mountains were very dark! Even headlights didn't help a lot. The views of the Pacific were breathtaking. The roads were pretty good in some places but bad in others. Like other countries of Central America, driving was hazardous because of the amount of foot traffic, animals, and bicycles sharing the road.

Our entrance into Honduras was very frustrating. We didn't have enough cash to pay the usual charges for completing the paperwork required to enter the country but at last they agreed to take a traveler's check. However, when I was getting the checks out of my glove compartment, I couldn't manage it without them seeing me do it. That came back to haunt me.

We stayed at a very nice hotel that night, and they had two guards so they told us our cars were safe on the street in front of the hotel. At about 8 PM I went to get something out of my car and it had been broken into. I was devastated! Where were the guards? Not being used to a vehicle with a sun roof, I had left it open so it was easy to reach in and open the door. Bill said that was just as well because they would have broken the lock otherwise.

Many of my things were strewn on the street but it was clear they were not interested in my music! My tapes were all there. The women from the hotel were appalled at what happened. They looked up and down the street and retrieved most everything but the traveler's checks and my CB radio. Of course I was able to cancel the traveler's checks just like they advertise in the TV ads, but it did cause some anxiety and inconvenience. The CB was not a great loss because most of my messages to Bill were "turn off your blinker, Bill!" I believe that someone at the border had noticed where I put the traveler's checks and followed us to our hotel, not realizing that they would not be able to cash them.

The next day we headed for the Nicaraguan border. The road was good all the way. Bill said it had been built by the U.S. army at the time of the contra war. We were stopped twice by the Honduran police, and they fined us both times. The second time was for not wearing seat belts. When I demonstrated that mine was firmly fastened around me, he paid no attention. Like most places in Central America, the police are paid a pittance so they make it where they can and gringos almost always have money to spare!

Nicaragua at last! However it was the worst border crossing yet. Perhaps it was because I was going to live in the country, but the paper work and delays were horrendous. Since my things had to go into a warehouse to wait to pass through customs, and the warehouse was in Managua, I was required to have a *custodio* ride with me all the way. I suppose they thought I might stop along the way and sell all I brought!

It was a pretty quiet trip because the *custodio* didn't speak any English and my Spanish was still pretty rudimentary. However, he did make me understand that he needed bus fare to return to the border!

When we finally arrived and got unloaded at the warehouse, it was 8:30 PM and we decided to go to my friend Grant's guest house for the night. We just showed up at his door but he was expecting us – a real surprise! Apparently Chris had informed him that we would likely do that rather than drive another 2½ hours at night to San Juan del Sur. He was right!

4

After we had had a good visit with Grant and Maggie, who was still living in Grant's guest house, we left for San Juan. Chris had a sailboat cruise that day, so we went down to greet him on the dock. He was very happy to see us finally in San Juan. Since Leslie had moved to San Marcos to teach English Literature at the university, I took over her room. Chris had fixed it up very nicely and it was quite comfortable.

We shared a bathroom, working out signals for when the bathroom was occupied, which worked most of the time. I remember once I was preparing to take a shower and the light was off, which meant it was not occupied. I entered the bathroom naked and lo and behold, the door to the other room was open and Luis Estrada, our friend from Managua, was standing there. I think he was much more embarrassed than I and quickly closed the door. So much for house rules! I was a bit more careful after that.

The next day we took a tour of the property, and Bill and I were very impressed. It had a wonderful view of the ocean and town as it was situated on a hill to the east. Chris shared some of his ideas about our building and it was wonderful to finally be able to talk about it and not just dream.

Perhaps I should say a little about this town of San Juan del Sur to which I was so drawn. It's a small fishing town located on the south Pacific coast of Nicaragua. Its population is around 18,000 or so which includes the heart of the town clustered around a horseshoe beach on the ocean, and the outlying areas with many small villages.

San Juan del Sur

Fishing had been the major source of income here for many years. At one time the port was used for loading and unloading cargo from other countries, providing jobs for the local men. By the time I arrived, the port had been closed and fishing was less and less productive. Many people were making their living through the service industry – restaurant/bars, small variety stores in the front of their houses, and working for the wealthier residents as housecleaners, gardeners, or watchmen.

What struck me most was the feeling of community – people were very friendly, sat out on their porches or the sidewalk in front of their houses in the evening, and called out to us and others as we passed by. It made me think of the days when I was a child when people would do the same thing. There was no TV or air conditioning to give us a reason to stay inside. It was very pleasant to sit on your veranda and enjoy the cool evening with family or friends.

Another important factor was the sheer beauty of the area. I had never lived near an ocean so it was a thrill to walk on the beach and experience the sound of the waves crashing on the shore and to watch the pelicans diving for fish. I had never realized that the ocean changes every day – a living thing. Somehow it makes you think about your own insignificance in the face of such magnificence and power. I have never tired of the scene and in fact have a view of it from my front porch. Friends often come to enjoy the sunsets with me.

On the beach in San Juan del Sur

Our first meeting with the architect for our project was on February 9th. He was from Columbia but spoke good English and we were able to share some ideas. He said we should be able to begin construction in about six weeks. We thought we were near to getting started so were very enthused. More good news – Luis called from Managua to say that I would be able to pick up my things from customs later in the week. It would feel more like home when I had some of my own belongings around me.

When we went to the customs warehouse, we were informed that the Montero should have been impounded, along with my other things until it passed customs. We were obliged to leave it with them so they could determine if it was really a 1990. Anything older was not allowed in the country to prevent old "clunkers" from being brought in adding to the considerable pollution that was being caused by the explosion in car ownership and taxis in the 1990s. Of course all the papers I had stated 1990, but apparently they had to determine that for themselves.

They also had to assess its value – they would not believe the sales document that stated the price as $8,500. Their assessment was about $7,000 higher so I had to pay import tax. When I complained, the official said, "It could have been higher!" Another problem was the engine number. Everyone in the world seems to accept the VIN (vehicle identification number) except Nicaragua. It was difficult to find, even though the manual showed where it supposedly was. We ended up bribing several officials before it was officially licensed in Nicaragua.

Bill left us to return to the States, but he would return frequently in the years to come for visits and to bring items for us and our employees. He drove a different vehicle every time, either to sell (with Chris' help) or donate to some needy organization. Sandra George and John Detwyler, investors in the project, arrived for their first visit and were pleased with the property Chris had chosen. They had many questions about the project which Chris must have answered to their satisfaction because they left talking as if they would invest additional funds. We were very hopeful.

It was time to start studying Spanish again. My friend Mae Ylagan in St. Louis had loaned me some cassette tapes to help me learn. I listened to them while driving down.

They were not the best because the instructors were not native Spanish speakers and spoke with an English accent. Chris thought they were pretty amusing, and not the best way for me to learn. He advised me to begin classes with Nelly Reinert, a woman from the Faro Islands in the North Sea near Scotland, who had lived in Nicaragua for some years and been married to a Nicaraguan. She spoke several languages including English and her spoken Spanish sounded almost like a native. Rather than dwell on grammar, which I had studied the first time I was here, we concentrated on reading articles in Spanish, translating them and then discussing them. It helped with my comprehension and my pronunciation.

I was timid about speaking to others in Spanish and it took some time for me to get up the courage to try to communicate. I didn't want to appear stupid. I continued to have trouble understanding what people said to me so we tried listening to songs in Spanish since I really enjoy music. Unfortunately that didn't help. To this day, I still have difficulty understanding everything said to me, and some people are much harder to understand than others. Chris' friend Luis told me the same is true for him with English, which he was doing his best to learn.

Chris persuaded me that we should buy more land. I was reluctant to agree because I felt we should concentrate on getting the hotel built. However, he was able to make his point that as San Juan became more of a tourist attraction and a place to make good and reasonable investments, people would build around us. He believed that we needed a buffer. This was a conversation we had several times over the next couple of years, and he always prevailed. I think the fact that he was a lawyer worked to his advantage! Development occurred as he predicted and we have been glad many times for the protection we have around us.

My sewing ability was put to the test very quickly when Chris requested a new sail cover for the boat. I had brought my sewing machine with me but this project was difficult on my small machine. The material was thick and hard to handle and really needed a powerful commercial one. Two of the women employees from the boat helped me and we made the best of it, but not without some frustration. It was the first of many things that Chris asked me to make – dust covers for electronic equipment, cushion covers for both the sofa and the boat and when we were ready to open the hotel, I sewed bedspreads, curtains, etc.

He was very anxious that I incorporate quilting into my sewing and urged me to teach some of the local women. I was reluctant for several reasons. I didn't feel my language skills were sufficient, I hadn't had much experience myself, and I felt that quilting is a European and North American art form, not Central American. I finally agreed to try it myself, and it has provided me with a whole new outlet for my creativity and challenged my sewing skills.

During those years I usually walked on the beach every day. I found the litter very distressing. Plastic bags have been a curse to Central America. Although plastic bottles are equally bad, soft drink and beer companies continue to use returnable bottles so it lessens the impact. The local people used to use banana leaves to wrap food. When they were done, they could throw them away because they are bio-degradable and also good eating for the animals. Plastic is not! I usually collected several bagfuls while walking and disposed of them in the nearest trash can. However, these were few and far between because they were often raided by animals looking for food or were carried off by someone who wanted a trash can for his/her own use. This problem of litter concerned me a lot and I puzzled over how to deal with it. I felt that if we could teach the children that it was unsightly and unhealthy, perhaps we could make a difference.

Many people have asked me over the years about what I do all day. It seems that if you are not actually doing some kind of work, you must be bored and at loose ends. In our culture work defines who we are. Not here. It's a refreshing concept. However, when I want something done quickly and on time, my North American frustration sets in. I often say that I love the pace of life here, so I have to accept the other parts that accompany it. Here it happens all in good time!

The part of me that was brought up to be a lady and learn all the crafts that are considered women's work, like sewing, embroidery, knitting, etc. has come in handy here. I have many projects, changing constantly. One that kept me busy at first was making small sculptures out of shells and driftwood I found on the beach when I went walking. And of course, I practice my dulcimer every day.

Our progress on the hotel was very slow. The architect just didn't seem to be able to produce what we wanted and was difficult to pin down as to a time-frame. All we seemed to be doing was spending money! One of our immediate needs was a person in charge of construction. Neither Chris nor I had any experience with building so we needed someone with expertise in that area. We approached two young men from Australia who were supervising the building of a house for our friends, Marie and Richard, but after several weeks of consideration, they turned us down. Another disappointment!

Axel, our construction boss, presenting one of the workers with a certificate of recognition for 5 years with the organization

Another man, Axel Meisengeier, was recommended to us. He had come from East Germany to help a friend build a hotel here and had construction experience in Nicaragua and back home in Germany. The only drawback was language. He didn't speak English, we didn't speak

German, and although Chris' Spanish was good, Axel's was not. However, we worked it out by asking our friend Marie, an Austrian, to act as translator. Axel was with us for eight years. Early on I can remember trying to speak to him in my poor Spanish and him trying to understand and respond in his poor Spanish. Even though the workers were very polite, I could just imagine them laughing at our attempts to speak THEIR language!

Once Axel began to work for us, some preparatory work began. The land was cleared, a *bodega* (storage place for materials) was begun and digging (manually) was started to house concrete tanks for water storage. City water was available and potable but not always reliable and so we had to plan for outages, particularly when we had guests in the hotel. During this time we made many visits, looking for ideas, to other hotels and to places with architectural details that interested us. We also visited La Paz Centro where roof tile was made. This was also the home of the team that built *ranchos*. We felt we wanted to incorporate both into our plans for the hotel.

A *rancho* or *palapa* is a type of building common here and in other parts of Central America (and the world), where there are palm trees and a warm climate. It is constructed with large, very tall tree trunks for roof supports and the roof is made of palm leaves. These men were real pros and when they were finally working on ours, they looked like a high-wire act. It seemed the waiting period for construction was over. We were wrong!

5

Because we had traded away Chris' old truck in one of the land deals, we felt we needed a replacement to do the heavy work and hauling for which we didn't want to use the Montero, which we had managed to extract from Customs after three weeks. We decided to buy a new Hyundai *camionetta*. A *camionetta* is a double cab pick-up. We felt it could do the job, although it did not have 4-wheel drive. Our intent was to only use it for hauling materials in town and to and from Managua where the roads were relatively good.

We discovered one of the big disadvantages of the model we bought was that it had four small wheels on the back that would continually need new tires. We had to learn that the hard way! By buying the second vehicle however, it freed up the Montero for me to use from time to time to take short trips with my friend, Maggie. I now had a

Nicaraguan drivers' license so could legally drive in Nicaragua.

Driving in Nicaragua is always an adventure, and we had a number of them. One Easter we decided to go to a popular resort of Nicaraguans, Trapiche, just outside of Managua, and we each enjoyed one beer while we were there. From there we went to check out a hot springs we had heard about near the town of Tipitapa. As we were driving through the town, I had the uneasy feeling that we were on a one-way street. Sure enough we were, but before we could correct our error, a policeman stepped out into the street and pulled us over. Unfortunately, when he looked at my license he pointed out that it had expired. Being fairly new to Nicaragua's licensing laws and finding the license itself somewhat difficult to read I didn't know that it even had an expiration date. Having had a driver's license for more than 50 years you would have thought I would have realized that every license has an expiration date.

He said we were to follow him to the station where I had to talk with the captain. The captain asked me if I had another license, and I did, from Missouri, but it had expired as well! Fortunately he was in good humor, and perhaps because I was an old white-haired lady he let us go without even a fine. However, his parting words were "It's not a good idea to drink when you are driving, particularly since it is Semana Santa."

Semana Santa (Holy Week) in Nicaragua is a time for celebration. There is a lot of reckless driving due to drinking, so to avoid an accident he felt I needed to have my wits about me. Of course, he was right even though I had drunk only one beer. I must admit I felt a little chagrined but also very lucky to get off so easily.

In San Juan del Sur we had our share of adventures as well. One day we made a trip out to Marie and Richard's house in the *campo* (country). They had had a problem with their truck in Managua and were not able to make it home that night, and since they had several dogs, they asked us to go to their house and feed them. It was during the rainy season and the roads were not good in the best of times. Fortunately, we had 4-wheel drive and set off to take care of the dogs. As we neared their house the road deteriorated even more and we came to a spot where the rain had dug a deep trench in the middle of the road. There was a farmer's house nearby with a yard that I thought we could ask to use, but Chris (typical male) decided we could make it – and we did, the first time.

However, when we left the house to return home, I again suggested the farmer's yard, but Chris was determined that he could straddle this trench another time. I was nervous so got out of the vehicle to watch and sure enough, as Chris was maneuvering over it, the rear wheel of the truck slowly slipped down into the trench and tipped and he had to climb out the driver's window.

We were wondering what we should do when out of nowhere came the farmer and several companions. They took in our predicament and began placing boulders in the trench for the truck to get some traction. One of them returned with a pair of oxen, hitched them to the front of the truck, and lo and behold, the truck popped right out. Needless to say, we were very appreciative, but we learned that it is not uncommon to receive help from the people who live in the *campo*. They are very willing, and in fact, probably enjoy seeing gringos needing THEIR assistance.

As time went on, we were increasingly concerned about money. With all the delays, it seemed to fritter away. We still hoped to be able to complete our project with investor money so we began to reach out to folks we thought might be able to help. We were fortunate that Bill Parsons, a friend of Grant's, and Harold Weise, a friend of mine from St. Louis, agreed to invest some money in our work. That gave us a little breathing room. We also were introduced to a friend of a friend, Jack Brown, who convinced us that he would have no trouble at all finding people who would be falling over themselves to invest. He did bring a few people to see the property and talk with us but unfortunately Chris and I were the only ones that he sold on the project! He did help us put together some information about our project to share with prospective investors which was very helpful. But one day he disappeared without finding one investor for us and we only saw him fleetingly after that.

We were becoming increasingly dissatisfied with our architect. We were not happy with his ideas and he did not want to try to incorporate ours. He was not reliable when it came to deadlines, and time is money, so finally we had had enough and told him we no longer wanted or needed his services. It was not a very amicable parting but we felt we needed to make a change if we were ever going to complete the project. Fortunately, several years earlier, Chris had met an architect from Mexico who was now living in Managua and he agreed to consider our project. We met with him several times and although we didn't care for his first design, the second time he came up with one that incorporated many of Chris' ideas. We decided to work with him and his plan.

Finally we began to make some progress. Axel continued to work on the infrastructure – building water tanks, digging a well, building many retention walls, and doing the preliminary water and electrical lines. Our first well never did produce water so we had to find a different and better location. We kiddingly referred to the first one as "Chris' folly."

Before the end of the year, we had started to lay the foundations for the service buildings and to seek bids for the swimming pool. We had decided to use adobe bricks for the walls of our primary buildings, so the challenge was to find a place that made them. Our soil didn't have the right properties. Adobe is relatively cheap, easy to work with, and has good insulating properties.

Our architect, Pepe Tercero, found a place near Nandaime, a town about an hour's drive away, and we made a trip there to see their work and determine if it was the quality we wanted. It was an education to see grown men playing in the mud! Actually, it is somewhat of an art.

The soil is mixed with water in a shallow pit and straw is added by the men who knead it with their bare feet. Once it has been thoroughly mixed it is placed in wooden molds and left to dry in the sun. I asked the supervisor how he knew when it was ready for the molds. Like many artisans, he said he just knew from the consistency of the mixture. We decided to buy from them, the only additional costs being transportation of the adobe to our property in San Juan.

Making adobe bricks

That year, 1998, I made my first of many trips to the United States to visit family and celebrate Thanksgiving with them. I chose to go to California this time because that's where my two boys and my one granddaughter (at the time) live. My children are widely dispersed in the U.S. and it is difficult to visit with all of them at the same time.

Fortunately, my daughter Diane, who lives in Jackson Hole, and Mary, who lives in St. Louis, were able to join us in California. At that time neither of them was married, but Diane brought her boyfriend, Dave, who subsequently became her husband. My other daughter from North Carolina and her husband were not able to make the trip.

It felt strange to be back in the States again after ten months in Nicaragua. You can just feel the pace of life pick up as soon as you arrive in the airport. I came through Houston and had a hard time dealing with the crowds, many with cell phones clamped to their ears (they were rare here at that time), and the number of choices available, particularly fast food.

On each trip back to the States, I came with a list of things to buy that we could not find in Nicaragua, or the price was too high. Often visitors would ask what they could bring as well. Chris always asked for chocolate and triscuits and sometimes artichokes if they were available. My usual request was for decaffeinated coffee. I got kidded a lot about living in a country that grows coffee and having to have it imported. Nicaragua does produce wonderful coffee but not decaffeinated. Their opinion, like many others, is why drink it if you can't have caffeine. Interestingly, Nicaraguans prefer instant coffee! As time went on, we needed less from the States as we could find just about everything we needed here.

Chris has always been an animal lover and had brought several cats and a little Yorkshire Terrier with him on the boat. By the time I met Mikey he was about 12 years old and had begun to have some health problems. While I was in California, Chris found a little mixed breed dog on a nearby beach, and since he seemed to be without home or family, brought him to our house. He was about three years old and a very friendly energetic dog. We named him Sufi from the Spanish word *suficiente* (enough), hoping that he was, as we had quite a collection of animals already. He was very good for Mikey, and we think he probably helped him live a little longer than he might otherwise have. I remember walking with the two of them on the beach. Mikey would be walking sedately behind, as befits an older dog, and Sufi would be so excited by the sand and water that he would come barreling towards us and bowl Mikey right over. Mikey seemed to take it all in stride.

The feeding place for the animals was on our front porch and it was amazing the assortment of creatures that enjoyed that food. Not only the cats and dogs but ducks, a wounded seagull and even a big fat toad. Each took their turn!

6

I was anxious that my family and friends visit and see what my life was like here in San Juan. We often had guests who were friends of Chris or came on some mission to aid the Nicaraguan people, and of course, Maggie, Luis, and Leslie were frequent visitors, but no one from my family and no U.S. friends had yet visited. In January of 1999, my good friend, Alice came for a two month visit. At the time she was in her mid-70s but seemed to have no trouble either with the trip itself or with living in close quarters with Chris and me for that length of time. In fact, she was surprised at how comfortably we lived.

Alice had spent time in Guatemala and apparently lived in fairly primitive conditions so expected it would be the same with us. She even commented on how well we ate – not just beans and rice! While she was here we did a lot of sightseeing and visited many places in Nicaragua together. She loved it all and left planning to return.

We were still living in town next door to our landlady, who was a very strange woman. She considered herself better than the many Nicaraguans who came in and out of our house. She would often complain to Chris about the "type" of people we allowed to visit. Yes, Nicaraguans have prejudices and different social levels just like any other culture and much of it has to do with appearance, unfortunately.

Light skin, the product of Spanish ancestry, is preferred. Nicaraguans on the east coast are descended from African slaves who escaped from other places in the Caribbean and are very dark. Everyone shows mixed heritage to some degree. Many have characteristics such as small stature, straight coal-black hair, and very chiseled features, indicating indigenous blood.

Our landlady and Chris had many disagreements over our Nicaraguan guests (and other things) so we began to think about moving. Eventually we hoped to have a place of our own on the hotel property, but we had other priorities at the time. It took until the end of 2000 for us to actually physically move to the property and even then, we did not have our own houses.

A Nicaraguan family was among the guests that visited us often. Gabriel, the father, worked with Chris in his boat business. He was a fisherman by trade and had a fairly good-sized motor boat. His job was to deliver crew and passengers to and from the sailboat, carry supplies, and accompany the boat in case of emergency. He and his wife, Petra, have three children – Nancy, the eldest, followed by Gabby and Jemma (pronounced Emma). The parents were very anxious that Nancy, who seemed to have a lot of promise, receive as good an education as possible and the parochial school in town had the best reputation. Chris offered to help Nancy financially, and, as a result, she attended this school throughout her primary and secondary years. She is now in her third year of university in Managua. Nancy has always enjoyed spending time with me, which surprises me given our age difference and my limited language skills. I think she feels that I am another grandmother in her life and she makes a point of remembering me on my birthday, at Christmas, and Mother's Day.

We continued to make slow progress on the hotel construction. We were again running low on money and felt we might have to close down and wait it out. Neither of us wanted to do that as we were worried that we would lose momentum that way. I began giving consideration to investing more money. I had some savings invested in the States but knew that there would be penalties for cashing them in. There would also be an income tax bite on my earnings. What if our project failed and I lost all my money? As I weighed all these considerations, I decided to ask Pepe, our architect, how much we could accomplish with my additional investment. After he had done some calculations, he felt we could complete the service buildings, restaurant, pool, rancho, and two hotel units. With that in mind, I decided to take the risk and cash in my savings.

Work began on the pool in June. The pool contractor told us it would be an eight-week process. Of course it didn't work out that way and in the midst of it all the contractor disappeared. Apparently he had run up many debts and his creditors were looking for him. Needless to say, construction was delayed. We considered changing to another contractor, but already had a fair amount of money invested in this one. We were up against that old dilemma: do you cut your losses and hire someone else or hang in there hoping things will improve? We did ask another company to give us a bid on finishing it and were astounded at how much they wanted. We decided to stay with the original contactor and hope for the best. We did like his design which was an infinity pool with the water falling down a waterfall to be recycled back to the pool. And he did eventually return.

Shortly after the pool was begun, the team arrived to start work on the rancho. This was a new experience for them because Pepe had designed it to be like a Mexican *palapa*. It was much taller (30 meters) than the Nicaraguan variety. Instead of having the typical sloping roof that came together at the top, this roof began the slope, then flared out to allow the wind to escape through openings in the sides of the flare. It was designed to prevent the wind from getting under the roof and lifting it off its supports. Long tree trunks to support the roof were delivered by truck, but given their weight (500 lbs each) the truck was unable to make it up the hill to the level where the rancho was to be built. Oxen were tried but couldn't get a grip on the cement driveway and kept slipping. Chris was beside himself watching the drivers using whips to urge the oxen on. Finally, it was manpower, ten men to a trunk, which managed to carry them up the hill. Nicaraguan men, as a rule, are not very big but they are amazingly strong!

Carrying the columns for the rancho

Once the supports for the rancho were cemented in place, work began on the inner structure of the building. It was made from more tree trunks, but much smaller, that were fitted together in a grid pattern. All this work was done in bare feet with no safety harness and caused me a great deal of worry. However, the men moved around those trunks like they were playing on a jungle gym and we had not one injury. The trunks were bolted together and then the joints were covered with what they called "noodles": rope wound in a very attractive manner.

Rancho under construction

When they finished the inside structure it was time for the roof. Palm leaves were tied in bundles and hoisted to the men above with a pulley system. They were then tied to the underlying structure. I can't tell you how many were required but they were amazingly quick. It took about six weeks for them to complete the whole job and when it was done it was an imposing sight which could be seen from almost anywhere in town. Chris was unhappy with it because he thought it looked crooked. They did some adjusting, not enough to fix the problem in Chris' view, but I felt that when building something with tree trunks that are not always straight it is difficult to end up with a perfectly square building. It's more of an art than a science.

Gardening had always been one of my hobbies when living in the States, so I decided to try my hand at it in San Juan. I had some successes but more failures. For some reason the seeds I brought from the States did not want to germinate here, and in one case a hotel gardener showed me ants carrying them off. I built a raised bed to try to outwit the ants and had better luck, but even then it was not very satisfying. I tried a vegetable garden, but the soil was very rocky and the plants did not do well. My cactus garden did better, but perhaps that is because cactus are native to Nicaragua. I hadn't grown the cactus from seed, but purchased them already started from a local *vivero* (nursery). Chris and his crew even brought some from the cliff above the beach where they took their boat passengers for lunch on the day-long cruise.

Growing wild on the property was a native species of cactus, pataya, which flowered once a year for one night. In some species the flower was as big as a dinner plate, mostly white with intense yellow centers. Incredibly beautiful! The fruit from this cactus is a vivid fuchsia color and is used to make a *refresco* (fruit drink) that is tasty and has the same beautiful color.

I had hopes of growing orchids but had mixed results with them although they seemed to grow in the wild very well. One of my best efforts was planting seeds of the malinche tree. They are called royal poinsiana in other parts of the world and are a beautiful tree with red/orange flowers in May, June, and July. They produce long seed pods which the squirrels love to munch on. Two of my seeds flourished and were transplanted to the hotel property where they grow next to my house to this day.

Another interest of mine is astronomy. Here, away from so many city lights, the night sky is magnificent. I am especially interested in the planets and for some years La Prensa, one of the newspapers from Managua, printed a weekly guide to the stars and planets. I read it each week to help me be aware of what astronomical phenomenon could be seen in our part of the world that week.

Not long after I moved to San Juan the guide alerted us to the fact that the Russian space station would be passing over our area. We were still living in town so that night I walked to the property to see if I could identify it. There was a young man serving as a *cuidador* (night watchman) and I explained to him what I had come to see. He listened to me in amazement as I tried to explain in my limited Spanish that the Russian space station was going to pass over and that it had people living and working in it. I'm sure he felt I was making it all up but we did see the blinking lights pass over us so I was thrilled. Since I was happy, he was too.

On my 70th birthday, Chris and my kids gave me a telescope, which I love, but I haven't had a lot of success with it. It's not an easy task to find something so far away in the vast expanse of the night sky. I find it hard to get my mind around how huge the universe is!

7

The end of the year 1999 found us still struggling to find ways to keep going. The extra money I had invested did not accomplish all that Pepe promised and we were to find, to our sorrow, that often things took longer and cost more than he had predicted. As an artist, Pepe was exceptional, but the more practical considerations escaped him. The pool was still not complete and what we had to show for all our efforts and expense didn't seem very much except for the imposing rancho that dominated the property.

Of course a lot of the work that had been done was infrastructure such as electricity, water, and retaining walls, and that didn't impress anyone very much, including us, even though we knew how much work and expense it involved and how vital it was to the whole project. At this point we were feeling pretty depressed.

Earlier in the year we had put together some promotional materials with the help of the elusive Jack Brown, which included our idea to create a fund out of our proceeds to support education for young people from San Juan. As I previously stated, I felt strongly that jobs and education would help improve the lives of the people here and could not help but benefit the future of Nicaragua. One day in December, 1999, a friend who had read our materials shared with us that someone she knew in the States had donated $2000 to purchase uniforms for children in San Juan and she suggested we handle it. Uniforms are compulsory here, even in public school, so children whose parents cannot afford a uniform do not go to school.

At first I was reluctant to take on the project as I didn't feel ready to begin, but realizing that this money would allow some poor children to attend school I decided to go ahead. We had been told by the school superintendent that 50 children in San Juan were not attending school so we agreed to start with them. Rather than buy the uniforms outright, I felt that we should find local women to make them so they would earn additional money for their household. The challenge then became to find the women.

I was directed to a local woman, Lilliam Reyes, who has worked with women for many years teaching skills to help them improve their lives. She had formed a women's cooperative and through that organization a feeding program for children had been established. Many classes such as sewing, cooking with soy products, and animal husbandry were being taught. Seminars dealing with self-esteem and domestic abuse, among other topics, were also presented to the local women.

One of their projects was a garden to grow plants for medicinal purposes. Lilliam had been trained as a natural medicine practitioner, which is a five-year process. Natural medicines were much more affordable for the local people who live on very little money per day. I remember going out to the *campo* with her and her daughter to administer anti-parasite medicine to the people in a small village. They had made up a large batch and administered it with a large syringe right into the mouths of the people waiting. They looked like little birds receiving food from their parents. Apparently this was a common practice.

Since she had a group of women she had taught to sew she eagerly agreed to take on this project. That was the beginning of our uniform project which is still active to this day and led to the establishment of Fundacion A. Jean Brugger. Chris had begun referring to our fund by that name and, although it seemed a little self-serving, I agreed.

School children receiving uniforms

Over the years almost 3,000 uniforms have been made and distributed. It is always a joy to accompany Lilliam and her assistant, Julia, when they deliver the completed uniforms to a school. The children are very excited because now they can attend school with their friends and not feel like outsiders. Often their parents come to the school that day to join in the celebration.

Since I am a nurse by profession, Chris thought I would want to get involved with the local health clinic, Centro de Salud, but I wasn't interested for several reasons. I had worked in the healthcare field for many years and wanted to do something different when I retired. In addition I found it very depressing to see the conditions under which the clinic staff worked. Due to under-funding from the government the clinics are poorly equipped and often lack common medicines. The staff does its best to help the patients, but I just felt there was no way that I, a North American dependent on modern methods, could adapt to the difficult situation.

It is not unusual for people in our area to die due to the lack of good medical care. There was a young woman we knew who died in childbirth from a complication that was treatable. Probably had she and the baby been in a modern hospital they both would have survived. I remember one instance when Chris was bitten by a cat and I felt he needed a tetanus shot. He went to the clinic and they didn't have any tetanus serum. He had to go to Rivas, the next nearest town that is a half hour's drive away. That is not an unusual experience, but at least needing a tetanus shot is not an emergency. He also had the good fortune to have transportation to take him there. Many local people do not.

Conditions are not much better in Managua, although hospitals there have varying reports as to their quality. Recently a new private hospital has been built and is staffed and equipped with the best trained physicians and the most up-to-date equipment. Unfortunately the poor cannot afford to go there. Many medical mission groups do come here on a regular basis and we are thankful for what they do, but they are not able to meet the day-to-day needs of the community. Emergency care is another concern since we are 2½ hours away from Managua and the hospital in Rivas is not very adequate.

I had enjoyed good health for many years but after entering my 60s I started experiencing elevated blood pressure. This triggered a heart irregularity that apparently is common in my family. I was referred to a cardiologist in Managua who was able to diagnose and treat the problem. I was reasonably confident in his ability because he came so highly recommended, but because he does not speak English, I felt I needed to seek the advice of a specialist in the U.S. who could explain things to me in English and answer my questions. As it turned out, the specialist concurred with the findings and treatment that my doctor here prescribed, so I felt much more confident that I was getting the proper care.

As the year progressed we began to finally have some good news. George and Kathy Knight from the Boston area decided to buy the land above the hotel, securing that boundary to the east. They had been coming to Central America for years as Kathy was a high school Spanish teacher and would bring groups of young people from her classes for a ten-day immersion experience in a Spanish-speaking country. Besides living in individual homes, they had a project to accomplish, such as painting a school, supplying the paint and contributing their labor.

After retirement, she and George were planning to spend half of the year living here and were anxious to get started building a house where they could live while in San Juan. They were also very interested in our hotel project and wanted to become involved.

One of their friends, Bill Rousseau, also decided to invest, the bulk of his money going to purchase the land south of the Knights that we wanted to set aside as a reserve for future generations of Sanjuaneños. Development is happening so quickly that we thought it was important to preserve some of the green space before it was all gone. As time went on, Kathy and George took a more and more active role in our project and became our very good friends.

Chris and I had discussed several times what we should call the hotel. He felt it should be something separate from Pelican Eyes, the name of his boat, but I thought that because Chris had gained a very good reputation over the years with his boat business it would help people make the connection between the hotel and him. One day he came back from a walk and suggested Piedras y Olas (rocks and waves). We compromised with Pelican Eyes Piedras y Olas or PEPO, and it stuck.

Many people have asked where the name Pelican Eyes came from. Chris tells me that when he and Jeff were sailing down the coast to San Juan, they trolled for fish. Often the pelicans would dive for the fish and end up with the lure lodged in their mouths. Rather than just cut the line, as most fishermen did, they felt they needed to do what they could to help the pelicans. One of them would hold the pelican, while the other would pull out the lure with pliers. Chris said it was an awesome experience to look the pelican in the eyes…and so the name.

Finally, several months into 2000, with the additional investment we had received from the Knights and their friend, we began to see some progress. The adobe was delivered and we stored some under the rancho roof and the rest in a nearby *bodega* (warehouse) until the construction workers were ready for it. Work was progressing on the foundations for the walls of the service buildings. Pepe had laid out the outlines of four hotel rooms.

We also made a trip to choose rock for the area around the pool and the floor of the rancho. There are a number of types of rock that are hewn out of the hills here in Nicaragua. The most common is called piedras canteras and is used a lot in construction. We had chosen a yellowish/white rock from an area north of us near Leon for the patio area and the waterfall connected to the pool. It is not only very attractive but extremely durable.

Pool under construction

About this same time, we had the very pleasant task of going to Managua to choose tile for the pool, which helped us feel that it really *was* going to happen. Our logo was to be made out of the same tile and placed on the bottom of the pool. We chose to make the lip or edging in Managua because it had to be molded. It was not available otherwise.

We began to feel that we might really have a hotel at last, but there were more obstacles ahead.

8

Chris was always on the lookout for pieces of land contiguous with ours that would enhance our property. I, on the other hand, kept reminding him that we had limited resources and had a hotel to complete. Somehow Chris was always able to come up with additional funds for land, which amazed me.

The "old man" as we called him, who had sold us most of our property, was now ready to sell his house and the land it was on – a small piece. As we contemplated how we might swing that deal, I suggested we talk with Sandra George and John Detwyler who I knew were looking for a place to retire in Nicaragua. Sandra has a congenital deformity that caused her to have one leg quite a bit shorter than the other and makes it difficult for her to climb stairs. Since our land is very hilly, we knew that there would be many stairs. This house was situated lower than the rest of the hotel property with a level access from the street, and looked to me like an ideal location for the couple. After some consideration, they concurred and purchased the house and surrounding land. They allowed us to use part of the house for offices and another part for Axel's living quarters. We were delighted.

Pressure from our landlady was increasing. We knew we had to make a move before the end of the year. In front of Sandra and John's house was another small property with two houses. Chris persuaded our friend, Greg Houston, a dentist from Kansas City, to purchase this piece. We planned to renovate these houses so that Chris could live in one and I in the other. They needed quite a bit of work so it was a race to complete them before we were evicted.

In late November 2000 Chris moved to his house, which was barely livable. I stayed with some friends who very kindly offered me lodging until my house was ready for occupancy. Little did we know I would be there for six weeks! When I finally made my move to the property, we still lived like we were camping out. I mentioned that to Chris, and he responded, "And I always hated camping." My good friend Alice returned for another visit in the midst of this and was a really good sport about the inconvenience.

A new tourist attraction, a canopy tour, was creating lots of interest, and Chris felt we should try it out while Alice was here to see if it would be something to recommend to visitors. A canopy tour is a ride on cables through the treetops of our tallest trees. The first one (subsequently there were others) was located on the side of one of our biggest and closest volcanoes.

This volcano, Mombacho, is one of two volcanoes in Nicaragua with a cloud forest. Clouds hang very low over the top of the volcano keeping everything very humid. The moisture allows for lush foliage on trees, with many branches covered with bromeliads such as orchids. There is a large variety of flowering plants attracting birds and colorful butterflies. Monkeys, salamanders, and reptiles live there, but are not often seen. A nature walk around the edge of one of the volcano's craters has been developed for visitors to enjoy the flora and fauna and the incredible view of the surrounding area. The last seismic activity was over 50 years ago but there are still chimneys, or fumaroles, which emit fumes from deep inside the volcano.

After we had walked around the crater we decided to investigate the canopy tour. Chris and Alice were eager to try it but I was nervous because of my fear of heights. However, I figured if Alice could do it and she was older than me, I should at least give it a try. They fastened harnesses around us and explained how to use the gloves they gave us to stop or slow our flight. We climbed a ladder to the first platform and I was selected to be the one to start. As it turned out that was a wise choice since I might have backed out after watching someone else.

The guide connected my harness to a pulley on the cable and rode with me, theoretically for the first time only. He did the braking and we landed on the first platform without incident. I was thinking that that would be it and was thankful that I had made it safely, if not happily. Little did I know that there were seven more! Chris came in behind me, followed by Alice. They were both thrilled with their ride.

The platform was not very large and I stuck close to the trunk of the tree because looking down would have been disastrous. In fact if I hadn't had to climb down the tree, I would have quit right then. I asked the guide to continue to go with me and made it through safely. I was thankful to put my feet on the ground and took much kidding from Chris and Alice about "hugging" my good-looking guide. For us older women that doesn't happen very often so we might as well take advantage of it when we can! I wished I could have relaxed and enjoyed it because it is a thrilling experience to fly through the trees like a bird or a monkey.

Speaking of monkeys, our animal population continued to grow both in numbers and varieties in spite of Sufi's name which indicated "no more." Besides him (Mikey had died several months previously) we added three more dogs and many more cats, whose numbers continued to increase once we moved to the hotel property. We fed them outside and as a consequence attracted all the strays in the area. Then they began to reproduce. We found little kittens everywhere! Chris could not find it in his heart to exterminate them, so our only recourse was to trap as many as we could and when they were old enough take them to the vet in Managua to be neutered. That helped, but we still come across kittens.

Over the years we collected monkeys, raccoons, coatis (related to the raccoon), wild pigs, and even an ocelot or two. We had hens, roosters, ducks, and geese. Needless to say, we had baby chicks as well if they could survive the predators within our animal population.

Chris is a fellow who can't say no when it comes to animals so when they were found or no longer wanted, they seemed to end up here. I managed to stay uninvolved with the animals until a baby monkey was brought to us and we felt we had to take it. Unfortunately people here have found that a way to make some money is to catch or trap wild animals and sell them on the street, or in our case, bring them to the door. It is always a dilemma whether to buy them or not, because it encourages people to continue, but yet we fear for the future well-being of the animal. Whenever possible, we return them to the wild. In this case, we knew the baby could not survive without assistance.

Never did I dream that I would be a mother to a monkey, but that is how it turned out. Chris was too busy and didn't have time to give her the care she needed.

As I fed her and played with her I was amazed at how similar monkey babies are to humans. The big difference is that monkeys will not let go even when they sleep and they have five appendages to hold on. Putting her down was a major undertaking and often took two of us. One would roll up a towel and then place it between Monica and the person holding her and hope she would let go and grab onto the towel. Most times it worked. Of course, it is a safety feature for a baby whose mother is flying through the trees, but for us it was a big problem.

Jean and baby monkey Monica

It takes some time for them to learn how to use their tails. One day as I was watching her play in the trees, she decided to jump but forgot her tail was still attached. She swung like a pendulum and looked pretty funny but it didn't faze her at all. Monkeys seem to be able to withstand pretty hard knocks. She has now grown up and has a baby of her own, but still continues her close relationship with Chris and me.

With the rancho erected, our attention turned to the bar, restaurant, and kitchen. We had originally planned to serve breakfast only, but over time that evolved into the idea for a full-fledged gourmet restaurant.

Chris hired a young woman who had run an excellent restaurant in Managua to help us list what was needed in the way of refrigerators, freezers, stoves, cooking utensils, dishes, serving trays, etc. We had talked with several carpenters about making the bar and decided on an S-curved shape with a concrete base and polished wooden top. It had indentations in the front to put lights or other decorative items. It was unusual and very attractive.

The restaurant itself was on two levels, the bar being on the lower one. We had a number of discussions about how to utilize the levels. My idea was to make the upper level the more formal one and the lower casual, being close to the pool. However, it turned out that both are the same – formal with tablecloths, cloth napkins, and good quality dinnerware and utensils.

We also began to talk about waiters and bartenders. Chris' choice was men for waiters and a woman for a bartender. Our hope was to find enough good candidates from San Juan. On the whole we were successful, but finding a woman bartender was difficult. Men's and women's roles are well-defined here and it is difficult to find exceptions to the rule. For example, most of the kitchen workers and all the housekeepers are female. The men are waiters, bartenders, and gardeners, plus of course, construction workers. One exception to the rule was a young woman engineer who was a supervisor in the construction area.

As time went on, we needed to hire more and more staff and now we are the biggest employer in the area, achieving another of my goals.

9

Fundacion A. Jean Brugger was growing but in a limited way. We were still supporting the Uniform Project which allowed many more primary school children to attend school, but we wanted to begin providing scholarships for high school and university students. Chris had already begun to support two young people and I was helping a young talented artist take art lessons. We were anxious to help more students by getting more people involved.

Rodney Barker, a lawyer from the U.S. and participant in the Sister Cities Project (five different cities in Spain, Germany, Norway, and the U.S. assist San Juan in a variety of ways) offered to help us acquire a 501(c)(3) designation so that U.S. donations could be tax-deductible. He agreed to become our treasurer and handle the contributions by depositing them in a bank account in the U.S. and sending letters of acknowledgement to donors. We were very grateful for his help. Since we did not qualify to be called a foundation in the States we became the A. Jean Brugger Education Project.

We set up a space for the Foundation in the administrative office and arranged for a young woman, Arlen Pomares, to work half-time as our secretary. She was a university student and had started working for PEPO some years before. Since Chris' time was taken up with hotel and boat business, I asked to take on the Foundation as my special project.

More and more people started to visit San Juan as tourists and with mission groups, and many heard about our Foundation. We began to receive donations which allowed us to help more students. Because we felt strongly that the whole community should benefit from these scholarships we required the recipients to accept some obligations. The students were more than happy to cooperate.

One of our first efforts to help the community was a litter pickup once a week, addressing my earlier concerns about the problem. The students each recruited youngsters ages 8-12 who worked with us for an hour each Sunday morning. We felt if we were able to raise the awareness in them that litter was unsightly, as well as unhealthy, perhaps the adults would follow. It is difficult to assess how successful we were with the children, but we did collect a lot of trash. Following each trash pickup, we provided juice and cookies for the workers. The cookies were in individual packages and believe it or not, after an hour spent picking up trash we would catch some of the children throwing their cookie wrappers on the ground! It takes time to change habits apparently.

A. Jean Brugger Educational Foundation students

As the year progressed we found ourselves short of money again. Our investor pool had pretty much dried up even though many people continued to be interested. We would get our hopes up each time, only to be disappointed as none decided to invest. Chris convinced me that our only option was to borrow. I wasn't happy about going into debt but there seemed no other solution to our ongoing shortage of capital. We had already gone through the steps to incorporate so felt that would be in our favor when we approached a lender. We did want to keep our money in

Nicaragua. Therefore, Chris approached several local banks about a loan. Only one was willing to consider us and at a pretty high rate of interest. We felt we had to go ahead. That started a process of preparing financial statements and projections. Each time when we thought we had provided all the information they needed, they came back with requests for more. It was very discouraging.

Reluctantly we laid off much of our construction crew but retained a group of about ten. The houses for Chris and me had been completed, at least enough to live in comfortably, so the small crew began to build the brick walkways and patios around the houses. Since it was the dry season it was incredibly windy and dusty. A lot of sand was used to mix with the cement that held the bricks in place, and it would drift into our houses at will. I would wake up in the morning with grit in my mouth and sand in my ears. One night it got so bad I slept with my umbrella open over my head!

Alcoholism is endemic to Nicaragua. Beer and rum are cheap and, as often happens among the poor, used to soothe those feelings of helplessness and inadequacy that living on the edge creates. Unemployment was over 50% so many men were at loose ends, their wives and mothers carrying the burden of supporting the family. Naturally this reinforced their feelings of hopelessness. Unfortunately we suffered when two of our most important employees began to show signs of alcohol abuse. We felt in a bind because Chris was afraid if we fired them, we would not be able to replace them. As I look back I think that was probably not true, but he was sure of it at the time. I was worried that not firing them would set a bad example for the other workers.

There was an Alcoholics Anonymous in town and several programs for drug and alcohol rehabilitation in Managua but nothing seemed to help until we found out about a *curandero* (medicine man) who lived fairly near. He had a reputation for helping both alcohol and drug abusers and after two visits to him, both of our employees stopped drinking and one is still staying clean. It was almost magical. Unfortunately others treated by him didn't have such positive results. A year or so later the *curandero* died and his wife took over, but never had as good results as he.

The two houses Chris and I lived in were opportunities to try out some of the ideas we had for the hotel. We wanted tile roofs and Chris insisted that he liked the looks of the bare tile from underneath, resting on the cross beams, so that's the way our roofs were made. They were put on during the dry season so we couldn't determine how they would perform when it rained. In May of that year we had our first storm and it was a doozie – thunder, lightning, and *very* heavy rain. At the height of the storm, I could hear Chris shouting that he was drowning in his house. Sure enough, water was everywhere and coming in fast and furious! With the help of Axel, our construction supervisor, we managed to cover everything and, thankfully, nothing was irreparably damaged.

That began a period of trial and error as we tried to retain the tile but find a way to make it weather-proof. We did not like the look of the corrugated metal that is used almost exclusively here, nor did Chris care for the imitation tile that was made from the same material. However they both did keep out the rain! After trying many things, including black plastic and tar paper under the tiles, our final solution was to use the metal and to disguise it on the inside with cane and the outside with tile. Unfortunately, we lost the look of the tile from underneath that Chris really wanted, but he agrees that the cane is very attractive. Since then, that is the way all our roofs are constructed and they do keep out the rain.

While we were waiting for some movement in our financial situation, Chris continued with his boat business. It meant a day away when he and the crew would sail the boat full of passengers down the coast to a beach where lunch was served. After several hours enjoying the beach and the water they sailed back to San Juan, often returning at sunset. I accompanied him regularly, but I am not a good sailor, needing pills to keep me from getting sick. However one trip was very special. From a distance we saw hundreds of birds diving into the ocean, so Chris took us over to see what was happening. Schools of sardines were swimming near the surface of the ocean, attracting the birds. Soon dolphins appeared to share in the feast. With birds flying overhead and diving for fish and dolphins surfacing and diving all around the boat it was spectacular!

From time to time we would see whales and one year when my family was visiting we came upon a whole pod of them. Everyone was excited and snapping pictures as quickly as possible. Reisha, my 3-year-old granddaughter, joined in the excitement even though she didn't understand what it was all about.

Pelican Eyes

A week later when a group of dental students was aboard, dolphins appeared in the water very close to the boat. Some of the students took advantage of the opportunity to jump in and swim with them. The dolphins were curious but not particularly interested in swimming very close to these odd looking sea creatures.

The busy season for the boat cruises is from November to April when many "snowbirds" came south to escape the cold weather. Unfortunately, other times of the year are spotty. At that time there were regulars like people from the various embassies who would often celebrate a holiday with a boat trip but not much business from tourists the rest of the year.

Chris was becoming quite busy with hotel details, both construction and financial, and I began to worry about how he could manage the boat and the hotel businesses, particularly after the hotel was open. Kathy, George, and I shared with Chris our concerns about his ability to be in two places at once and he grudgingly admitted that he should seek a boat captain to take over for him. This was a very difficult decision for him because the boat was his "baby." He was afraid he wouldn't be able to find someone he could trust who would care for the boat and insist on the same high quality of service his passengers were accustomed to.

Over time he was able to let go and recruit some very capable captains to do the job satisfactorily, even though the first one disappeared after three days. She either didn't really want the job or became frightened once she realized it was a big ocean out there. I think Chris missed the opportunity to get away from his worries for a day from time to time and of course, having sailed all his life, he did enjoy being out on the water. The cruises remain a very popular excursion for our hotel guests.

10

By mid-2001 we were getting desperate for funds. Same old story! We had still not heard from the bank. We had had several donations and borrowed from some friends, but it was not enough to see us through. A friend, who I'll call Bob, had told us about a group in England that was willing to finance projects such as ours. Bob was hoping they would lend to him and felt if we approached them jointly they would be more likely to finance his (Bob's) project as well as ours. The only drawback was they were asking for some money up front. That made us pretty skeptical. We told Bob we could not put any money up so if he still wanted to go ahead he would have to pay for both. Bob agreed, so we filled out all the papers required for the loan and mailed them off to England. As it turned out our instincts were right. After many promises, emails, and telephone calls this group never came up with any loan money and I don't know if Bob ever got his deposit back. We were thankful we had not fallen into that trap.

We were still hopeful that the loan from the bank might come through. They wouldn't say "yes" and they wouldn't say "no" so we were in limbo. As time passed we began to give up hope of ever receiving any money from that source.

In the fall of that year we met a man, Peter Gould, who would have a great impact on the direction our project took. He had come to Nicaragua looking for a good investment and spent some time in San Juan checking out various possibilities. He had heard about our project and after looking around and talking with us at length, decided our project was where he wanted to put his money. However, there were strings attached. He wanted to buy a small piece of land just to the south of our property and have Axel and our team build him two houses. One was to be a replica of the house Chris lived in, which he would use as his residence when he was here and the other just like the one I lived in, which he would use as a guest house. We greeted this proposal with enthusiasm because it meant a number of our construction workers could be rehired. Unfortunately, it didn't help much to move our project along.

In early 2002 we were still waiting on the bank. Chris had put incredible effort into trying to make it work and even the bank manager had felt it was pretty much a sure thing. However, he shared with us that the bank owners were much more willing to loan money to their friends and relatives than to people like us regardless of the merit of the project. Unfortunately that is the custom here and according to James Michener in his book *Caribbean* was a result of the Spanish occupation which became the norm for how to do business.

I had some family events to take the problem off my mind. My youngest daughter, Diane, had a baby in February, and I was there for the birth and for her daughter's first month of life. It is quite an awesome experience to be with your child when she gives birth. I found it more meaningful than giving birth myself! Dave (dad), sat over in the corner of the delivery room, however, hiding behind a paper until he heard the cry of his first child. Dave is a pretty laid-back guy, but you could tell by his expression how pleased and proud he was.

Later in the year, my oldest son, Ron, came to visit us in San Juan. He was the first of my children to come since we started the hotel project, and he seemed to be impressed with what we had done so far. A friend came with him, and we did a fair amount of sightseeing in spite of the rain. It was in May, the beginning of the rainy season so not unexpected. I can still see Ron and Bob in the back seat of the Montero, arms out the window snapping pictures with their digital cameras as we rode along. There is always a lot to see on the roads here and they were fascinated.

They are both scuba divers and so we contacted a group at Laguna de Apoyo, one of our volcanic lakes, and they arranged to dive there. It was their first dive in fresh water, but unfortunately the rain made it very murky so visibility was poor. Those lakes can be many hundreds of feet deep and are usually very clear. We also made a trip to Ometepe, the island in the middle of Lake Nicaragua. It has two volcanoes with a narrow strip of land in between and is a place that has retained its character in spite of the influx of tourists and technological advances. I think Bob's most memorable experience was when he ordered fish soup and it was served with the full fish, head out one side of the bowl, tail out the other.

Volcano Concepcion and the island of Ometepe

July was approaching and we had promised Peter that he could stay in his house when he came early in the month. It was far from ready. All the houses built as part of our project were turnkey, which means they were ready to move into with all the amenities in place. Chris put pressure on Axel and his team to finish their work. We made several hurried trips to buy furniture, appliances, mattresses, dishes, pots and pans, sheets, towels, etc. It was fun because we were spending someone else's money for a change. My job was to make the bedspreads and the curtains. We did our best, but unfortunately, Peter had to stay his first night elsewhere. He did not seem too upset and his pleasure on seeing his house made up for any inconvenience.

The Foundation was growing and prospering. We were still delivering uniforms to schools in the *campo* and increasing the number of scholarship students. I began putting together our first newsletters, but had to turn to Chris to help with layout since my computer skills were just not up to it. We had begun regular meetings with our students and, as my Spanish was still pretty rudimentary, Arlen led the meetings. Gradually she was assuming more responsibility and that pleased me because my hope was that she or another Nicaraguan could direct the Foundation in the future.

We had also begun to explore the possibility of becoming a legal foundation in Nicaragua. As with all types of official business here, it was a long complicated process, requiring information about the foundation, names and copies of passports or *cedulas* (identification cards) of our board members and of course, money! The application had to be approved by the Asemblea, the governing body of the country and published in their official records. As you might guess this was a multi-year process but finally we became a legal entity in 2005.

For the first seven years that I lived in San Juan I did not have my own kitchen. In some ways it was very enjoyable – a young woman, who came every day to clean and launder, made our lunch as well. The evening meal was usually leftovers. Chris and I took turns heating them up. From time to time, however, I got the urge to cook. Chris was particularly fond of chocolate chip cookies, so I made them occasionally as well as bread, pies, and cakes. These were things our Nicaraguan cook did not know how to make. I began to teach her some gringo-type dishes to include in the menus for lunch. She was eager to learn.

I did have one big frustration, however. Because Nicaraguans have very simple homes as a rule, they do not have kitchen cabinets or drawers to store things. They often have just a shelf to accommodate dishes, cooking pots, utensils, etc. Since they are in plain sight and easily found there is no need to separate or organize them. Faced with cabinets and drawers in our kitchen, they continued their practice of putting things wherever. The problem was magnified because we not only had our regular housekeeper working in the kitchen every day but whenever there was a cruise, the two women from the boat used the kitchen to prepare the food to serve on the beach. For me, who was used to "a place for everything and everything in its place" it was incredibly frustrating. I would spend five to ten minutes looking for what I needed and even then did not always find it. I reluctantly learned to live with it.

One of the celebrations that is very important here and elsewhere in Central America is the *quinceanos* (15th) birthday of a young girl. In July we helped celebrate the birthday of Nancy, the daughter of our closest Nicaraguan friends. It was a big affair which began with a mass in the church followed by a reception in the town community center. Nancy was dressed like a bride, except for her pink dress, and was escorted by her dad into the church. She was preceded by a group of younger girls all dressed in lovely dresses and carrying flowers. It was just like a wedding except there was no groom. Some would say that is an improvement!

Refreshments were served at the reception, including a multi-tiered birthday cake. I had helped transport the cake from where it was made in Rivas, and it was a challenge to keep it intact until we reached San Juan. Since there was no covering or other protection we all ended up with pink frosting on us. As with all Nicaraguan celebrations there was music and dancing until the wee hours.

In August, 2002, we had the first of a number of claims to our land. Land issues in Nicaragua became a problem after the 1980s. When the Sandinistas were victorious in the revolution of 1979, they established a socialist government. They were condemned by the U.S. for being communists. Many of the wealthy people fled to Miami because they were afraid that it would indeed become a communist state. Some industry was nationalized, such as utilities, but other private businesses were allowed to continue. There was free education and free healthcare. The literacy rate rose and the infant mortality rate dropped. Many peace and justice groups from the U.S. and Europe came to experience, participate in, and support this alternative to capitalism.

Part of the government's program was to seize some of the vacated property and portion it out to *campesinos* (small farmers) so that they could begin to grow their own crops. However, they did not follow the traditional legal requirements, so the recipients did not have the documents to claim ownership. After the Sandinistas were defeated in the 1990 election, people began to return to claim their land. Needless to say, this created many conflicts, some of which have not been resolved to this day.

When we purchased our land Chris had been very careful to be sure that all the proper procedures had been followed, but that did not prevent challenges. We continue to struggle with those problems. Each challenge requires a team of lawyers to negotiate with the claimants and ends up costing a great deal of time and money, not counting the stress it engenders.

A complicating factor is that investors and developers have come to take advantage of this new relatively untapped market, which has resulted in increasingly inflated land prices. Our land became very desirable and the development we had done only added to its value.

The most dramatic challenge occurred in the fall of 2006. An original San Juan family claimed they owned much of the land in town including ours and that of several other foreigners. They either wanted the land or $7,000,000. Many rumors were being spread around town and our employees were as upset as we were. Naturally they feared for their jobs.

A town meeting was organized by several employees to provide an opportunity for the mayor to explain to the people of the town what was happening. Over 1,000 people attended this meeting. Many positive speeches of support were made. Chris and I were both asked to speak, in Spanish of course, so I asked Arlen to put my sentiments into proper Spanish and I read it. Even so, it was pretty intimidating to speak in a foreign language in front of so many people for whom it was their native tongue. I was concerned that my pronunciation would be wrong and they wouldn't understand what I was saying. However, I needn't have worried as it was well received, probably because they were appreciative of the effort I had made. We were overwhelmed by the turnout and the many expressions of support and felt affirmed by the presence of so many of our friends, students, and employees.

11

At last we were able to borrow money, but not from the bank. While I was in the States visiting family, Chris called to say that a couple, who had made some money selling property here, was willing to lend us enough (we hoped) to complete the hotel. It was a good deal for them because they asked, and Chris agreed, to pay them the same interest as we would have paid the bank. It began to look as though we might finally have a hotel!

Our first homeowner, Peter Gould, had suggested to Chris that a way to raise additional money for the hotel would be to build more houses like his and sell them to investors. They could be rented when the owners were not here, and we would share the profits with them. Since it would be a good investment he felt there should be no problem attracting interested buyers. Chris liked the idea and was able to find an interested person who would loan us the money to build a speculation house to test the market.

Once we had the money from the loan we began to progress pretty rapidly. Foundations were built for the walls of the rancho and then the walls themselves. Finally some of the adobe we had had made so long ago was being used. I had told Chris that I wouldn't believe that we would have a hotel until the walls started going up, so it was with great pleasure that I helped place the first adobe brick.

The pool was open at long last. Although there was still some finishing to do and some problems to correct, we were able to swim and enjoy it. We were not the only ones! Some of our workers and their families, plus groups from town, seemed to feel this was a public pool and came often. We were not sure how to handle the problem. Our philosophy has always been to be as much a part of the community as we could, so we didn't want to erect barriers by denying access. The issue wasn't resolved until the hotel was open when we could legitimately announce that the use of the pool was for hotel guests only.

I had bought a bottle of champagne some months before to drink when the pool finally opened. George and Kathy were with us in the pool one day and George offered to go to the kitchen to bring it and some glasses for us to toast the new pool. When he removed the bottle from the refrigerator he discovered it had already been opened so of course the champagne was flat. The girls in the kitchen, thinking it was white wine, had probably used it for a chicken dish they often prepared. Imagine their surprise when they found out what it was! We laughed and drank it anyway. It made for a memorable occasion!

We were very interested in straw-bale construction and wanted to try it for our hotel rooms. This is a type of building material made from bales of straw, as its name implies. It's light-weight, easy to handle, and has all the same advantages as adobe – inexpensive, readily available, with good insulating properties. However, there was one drawback. It had to be well sealed so that rain could not penetrate and damage the straw. We heard of two Canadians who had the reputation of being experts in this type of building, so we arranged for them to come and do a workshop using our first four hotel rooms for hands-on experience.

Straw-bale construction

Foundations had to be built before they could start, and there were strict rules on how that should be done so that no water could seep in from below. It was the task of Axel and his crew to have them in place before the Canadians came. It was done to their satisfaction and the workshop commenced. Besides our own workers, there were several interested observers. Work progressed rapidly. It seemed like a miracle to see our first hotel rooms going up.

At about this same time, the walls of the service buildings were begun. The foundations had been built some time previously and the adobe was on site so work progressed quickly. We had some deterioration of some of the adobe bricks, which worried Chris considerably, but apparently they had made enough extra. The service buildings were originally to house the kitchen, the laundry, reception, and public restrooms. Since plans had changed over time, and we were to have a full-service restaurant rather than one to prepare just breakfast and snacks, it was apparent that the kitchen was too small. To make more room, we decided to move the laundry to another building which would be built near to the houses where Chris and I lived.

A young couple who were living in San Juan was very interested in helping design the kitchen. Brad was a graduate of a culinary school in the States, so we felt he had the expertise to guide us and arranged to have him work with us. The stoves, ovens, refrigerators, and freezers that he recommended were ordered.

It seemed we could begin to think about a grand opening celebration later in the year. As we thought about who we should invite and what kind of entertainment would be appropriate, I suggested we ask Norma Helena Gadea to perform. I had first heard her in concert in 1996 and had been a fan ever since. She sings traditional Nicaraguan music with such passion that even if you don't understand the words you can't help but be captivated.

One day Chris, Luis, and I were having lunch in a restaurant in Managua and she walked in the door. I was so astonished and said out loud "that's Norma Helena!" just like a teenage groupie. She heard and came over to our table and greeted me with a kiss on my cheek. I was really thrilled. Chris agreed that we should approach her about performing at our opening. We asked and she very graciously accepted. That was the first of her several performances at our hotel.

Kissing people when you greet them is a common practice in Nicaragua, but seemed very foreign to me, at least at first. When I arrived at the airport for my first visit to Nicaragua and was met by my friend, Maggie, and one of her priest friends, he kissed me. My first thought was "Why are you kissing me, I don't even know you!" My midwestern up-bringing was showing! I have since become accustomed to the practice and don't think twice about it.

One of our construction workers asked Chris and me if we would be godparents for his child. We were not sure what it entailed as this is a different culture, and often things are not the same as we are used to, but we agreed anyway, thinking it was probably just a formality. The ceremony was to be in the local Catholic Church on Christmas Day. We were surprised to discover that it was not just her baptism, but about 40 other young children's as well. The priest was difficult for me to understand so he may have explained what our responsibilities were, but I still didn't know. Chris didn't seem to understand either.

After the ceremony we were invited to their home where they had prepared a meal for us and family. They apparently expected us to spend the day with them as there was a party for our godchild planned for later. Since it was Christmas Day we had made other plans so had to leave not long after eating. I'm sure they were disappointed and confused by our apparent lack of understanding of their tradition.

Not unlike some other Nicaraguan children, our godchild was afraid of us, and it took several years before she was comfortable in our presence. She and her mother came to visit from time to time. Usually they were in need of help of some sort, most often money. Her father had lost his job and they were really having trouble covering even their food costs.

One day the two of them arrived with several of her other children. The mother was concerned because the older child had some kind of skin disease which caused a lot of itching. She had taken the child to the local health clinic but received no help so turned to me. As I examined her, I was thinking it might be a tropical disease that I had never seen before so wasn't sure what to do to help. I gave her ointment for the itching and some vitamins in case it could be caused by a vitamin deficiency. At least the vitamins could do no harm! I also recommended that she go to the local pharmacist for some antibiotic ointment because some of the "bites" were infected. As she was leaving she mentioned that one of the other children had a similar problem a couple of weeks before. The light dawned! It was chicken pox. Nothing exotic at all!

We did our best to help the family and provided gifts at the appropriate times such as birthday and Christmas. I know they were appreciative, but we never did receive anything in return, not even a birthday or mother's or father's day card....or even a "gracias." It has been a pretty one-sided relationship so far. Her mother is now working for us and seems much happier since she is more independent and has more self-esteem, so perhaps things will improve.

Chris informed me one day that the speculation house had been sold. A lawyer from Boston and a couple who were close friends of hers had decided to buy it together. Needless to say we were happy and relieved.

Chris had also succeeded in persuading two ophthalmologists who were here with a mission group to buy a piece of land just south of us and up a hill. It had a simple house on the property and had belonged to some Russians at one time, so it was called "the Russian house."

We were particularly pleased when the doctors decided to buy it because the family who lived there were not the best neighbors. Among other things they threw their trash down the hill towards us. We put up a fence, but all it succeeded in doing was catching the garbage and piling it up. This purchase caused the residents to move. We were not sad to see them go. It took a lot of time and work to clean up the property, and for awhile the house was used as a dormitory for our workers who did not live in San Juan. Eventually the house would be torn down and replaced.

12

2003 was a time of celebration and sorrow in my life.

My son-in-law Dave had given Diane a trip to Nicaragua for her birthday in January. A month later she, Dave, and their one-year-old daughter came to visit. Diane had visited me in 1996 and helped me make up my mind to embark on this adventure, but it was the first time for Dave and, of course, for Reisha.

They had not been informed that Reisha needed a passport to enter Nicaragua so there was a hold up at immigration. I was waiting for them in the terminal and couldn't understand why they didn't appear. I was worried because I knew that neither Diane nor Dave spoke Spanish and would have difficulty understanding the problem. Finally a customs official who could speak English was found, and the problem was resolved by agreeing that they would go to the U.S. Embassy and apply for a temporary passport before leaving the country.

Reisha celebrated her 1st birthday while here and enjoyed everything until she put her finger in the candle flame! Since she was just learning to walk and to master keeping her balance, riding over our rough roads in an unstable vehicle was more than she could tolerate. Of course she made her discomfort well known and there was nothing anyone could do to comfort her. We all suffered with her, but especially her mama.

The day before they left we went to the Embassy for her passport, and then on to immigration to have it stamped. We left it until the last day to go because it saved us an extra trip. Since it's a five-hour round trip drive to Managua, we tried to make as few as possible. They had an early flight the next day, so we planned to stay overnight in a hotel near the airport. Chris, who was a warden (local contact for the embassy) used his influence and Reisha's passport was waiting for us when we arrived at the embassy. All we had to do was have a passport picture taken.

The immigration process didn't go so smoothly. Normally when you enter Nicaragua as a tourist, they allow you to stay for 90 days. In the process of stamping Reisha's passport the immigration clerk had to figure out how many days she had been in Nicaragua and subtract that number from the 90 allowed. It was a laborious process. I kept saying it didn't matter because they were leaving the next day. That did not deter her one moment. Bureaucracies are the same everywhere it seems.

In May I got the news that my cousin Sue had died of liver cancer. Sue and I were close in age; she was the nearest thing I had to a sister. We had spent many summers of our youth together as she lived next door to my grandmother with whom I stayed for several months when school was out. Even though she had not been well for some time, she was not one to go to the doctor, so no one knew how serious it was. Her husband, Jack, had succumbed to lung cancer a year or so before. It seemed odd that both of them should die of cancer, but they were long-term smokers so that may have been at least part of the reason.

As my children turned 40 we agreed as a family to celebrate each person's birthday with a family reunion. In September we gathered in Cuba, Missouri, for Diane's 40th. We were at the cottage of a friend of Ron's who had been considered a part of our family since he and Ron were in second grade. The cottage was on a lake, and since the weather was mild everyone enjoyed playing in the water during the day. In the evening we tried out our voices with Mark's karaoke set-up. One evening we played dominoes and I, surprisingly, was one of the winners. It must have been beginner's luck as I didn't remember ever having played before. As is usual with our family gatherings, we had a wonderful time catching up on each other's lives and just enjoying being together.

While I was in the States, I visited Maggie and was pleased to see how well she was doing after her chemotherapy following a diagnosis of lymphoma. She was to return to Nicaragua in a month or so. I also visited my good friend Alice who was not doing well at all. She was very thin and had no appetite. We both knew that this was probably the last time we would see each other, so it was a bitter-sweet visit. Alice died a month later of liver cancer, which surprised me because I had been told previously that she had hepatitis. However, according to her family her last days were comfortable, without pain, and she died very peacefully. I was so thankful that I had made the effort to visit.

The hotel was progressing. The windows, doors, and floors in both the rancho and the service buildings were complete. Chris had chosen furniture for the restaurant and bar. It was made in Managua of decorative wrought iron with cloth covered seats on the chairs and bar stools. The fabric has had to be changed a number of times due to fading from our strong sunlight and people sitting on them with wet bathing suits.

The next step was to choose fabric for the tablecloths and napkins. Chris had very definite ideas about what he liked, and since I had no strong preferences, we selected the one he chose. It was left up to me to make them and the napkins. Lilliam, the woman in charge of our uniform project, and her daughter agreed to help me with the sewing. I did all the cutting, thinking they might not measure accurately, but guess who made the mistakes! I should have had more faith.

Things were coming together at last. The kitchen equipment had been delivered and Chris and Brad enjoyed placing it in the most convenient and efficient locations. I was working on bedspreads for the hotel rooms. Chris was very taken with my quilting, so we designed a bedspread with a strip of quilting down one side. It was unique and I received many compliments.

About this time, a woman by the name of Karen Dovey was visiting San Juan and was very impressed with our project. She talked with Chris about building a house for her like the ones we had already built. There was a bluff to the north of the hotel which had been purchased by our friend, Greg Houston, for his future home. Chris persuaded him to trade that property for another on site so it was agreed to build Karen's house there.

It seemed there was no turning back. Chris felt strongly that building investment homes was a way to complement the income we would receive from the hotel and allow us to continue to expand and improve our facility. I wasn't so sure. I felt there might be other options, but we never took the opportunity to discuss it as Chris was so convinced his decision was the only way to proceed. We would go on to build many more houses. Unfortunately it led to a disruption in our partnership, but not in our friendship.

Chris and Brad decided to have a trial dinner with guests selected from the community. It was an opportunity to try out the kitchen, Brad's culinary talents, and get some preliminary assessment of our restaurant and service. On the whole it seemed to go well, but since Chris' standards are very high, he felt there was room for improvement. That's probably only natural since everyone involved was new, and the dinner was meant as a way to see what additional training was necessary.

Apparently Brad had not intended to stay with us any length of time. Once he had gotten us up and running he decided to move on to other things. He had asked a friend, Monica, from the States, to come and work with him and he gradually let her take over. Between the two of them, they trained a Nicaraguan crew to work in the kitchen. Brad's wife, Stephanie, who had attended a bartending school, was teaching our newly hired staff to make drinks. She and Monica, with Chris' input, set about training the waiters. It was amusing to see them practice carrying trays with plastic bottles of water, which wouldn't break if they slipped off the tray.

The rush was on to complete everything by grand opening December 13th. But the hotel rooms were not ready. We wanted to be able to allow tours at the time of the official opening so that people would have a glimpse of what we had worked so long and hard to accomplish. As before, pressure was put on to complete the construction, and it came down to the day before for us to make up beds, hang towels, and make it look as ready for occupancy as we could.

My son, Ron, had come to represent the family at the opening, and we had asked him to bring a suitcase full of bedding and towels. We had ordered some from a hotel supply house over the Internet but they were held up in Customs and finally sent back. I persuaded Ron to help me make beds, and together with Chris we managed to get the rooms looking as presentable as possible. Needless to say, there were still details to be finished, but for all intents and purposes, they were ready.

Norma Helena Gadea

We had invited Nicaraguan friends and associates and members of the foreign community to be our guests for the opening. We served drinks and hors d'oeuvres. Norma Helena, accompanied by her long time guitarist, Eduardo Araica, provided the entertainment. She always supplied her own sound system and technicians to assure the quality that she required. It's a good thing she did because the sound system my son-in-law had purchased for us in the States had not come. It was held up in Customs (our nemesis) and took even longer because it came with the wrong invoice. You can imagine how angry that made all of us!

Everyone seemed to love Norma Helena, in spite of a sudden thunderstorm and downpour in the midst of her performance. As she sang many familiar Nicaraguan songs there was a lot of singing along and dancing to the music. Nicaraguans are a very responsive audience. It's fun to see them interacting with the entertainers...and the entertainers enjoying it just as much.

For us, the only drawback was the food. Monica had prepared several choices and one of them was barbecued ribs. It's always difficult to hold a glass and eat from a plate, but barbecued ribs made it almost impossible. Not only were your hands messy from the sauce but there was no place for the bones when you were done. There also didn't seem to be enough food for everyone. Chris was not amused, nor was I. She and Chris were not getting along anyway and this was the last straw. Following the opening they mutually agreed to her resignation.

LBee Bushey, a chef recommended by some friends, came to the rescue, jumping right into Christmas preparations. She was with us until December, 2009, and made our restaurant *the* place to eat in San Juan because of the excellent food….and there was always plenty of it!

We started accepting guests in the new year. One of my long-time friends from St. Louis, Carolyn Hileman, was among the first. She had invested in the hotel early on and was a great advocate for it and the Foundation. She was impressed with everything and thoroughly enjoyed her visit, as did I. Finally, after much work, worry and frustration our hotel was open!

Restaurant and bar

13

My older brother Bill died in April of 2004. His wife had been ailing for a long time and much of her care fell to him. At the urging of his family he had successfully transferred her and himself to a nursing home the year before. As they had adjoining rooms, she was quite happy. My brother was free to come and go as he liked so was able to play golf weekly with his friends. His health was not good and her care had taken its toll. He died quietly in his favorite chair in front of the TV. Even though I knew he was not well and worn out from taking care of Marj, I was still not prepared for his death. He and I had been particularly close when we were young and still had a special relationship.

Marj lived for another three years. Fortunately, a year before she died my daughter Mary and I stayed with my niece for a week and visited Marj every day. Mary made a little gift for her each day and proclaimed the week we were there "Brugger Week." Marj and I had known each other since we were children, so we had a lot of reminiscing to do. It was a special time for both of us.

The Foundation was taking more and more of my time. We had set up an office in my house, and Arlen was working every day. She was very computer-savvy and was able to take over Chris' job of helping me with the newsletter. We held monthly meetings with the students and they were planning many projects to fulfill their community service obligation.

During *Semana Santa* when many Nicaraguans flock to the beach, we always had a great influx into San Juan. Needless to say, the garbage and litter increased incredibly. We decided to prepare litter bags with a note urging visitors to put their refuse in the proper containers and the students handed them out as people came into town. They gave out over 3,000 bags. I don't know if it made any difference, but perhaps our efforts raised some awareness. Hopefully it didn't add to the litter problem!

During my walks around town, I would see many older adults sitting on their porches staring off into space. I had worked with older adults in St. Louis and felt there must be something we could do to improve their lives. Chris and I had always hoped to find ways to invite the local people to share our beautiful place and wonderful view. When I came up with a plan to bring some of them up for coffee and a roll one morning a month he agreed. Arlen was excited about the idea and suggested that the students help.

That began our *Ancianos* program which has continued ever since. We began with fourteen in attendance and it has grown to more than 100, about a third of them men. The coffee and roll I originally suggested was expanded to include a full lunch. There was often entertainment and they played bingo almost every time. When we had few players we could play until everyone won a prize, but as our numbers grew we could no longer do that. People were generous about contributing prizes, but coming up with over a hundred each time was more than we could manage. We compromised by playing until there were about ten winners. There was always music and many of them danced and sang. What more could anyone want!

Ancianos

The *ancianos* expressed their appreciation in many ways. A statement several of them made touched me the most – many thought they would never see some of their friends again and were thankful that we offered them the opportunity to renew friendships and enjoy each other's company….and they *do* enjoy!

A major concern for us was that we had always intended to be part of the community and not isolated up on the hill. However we were aware that the prices for our food in the restaurant put us out of the reach of most of the local people. It was suggested to us that we hold concerts at the hotel and encourage many from town to attend. The ticket prices would be affordable for most, and LBee was willing to prepare a special menu so that the cost of food would not deter anyone from coming.

Most of the popular artists planned their concerts in Managua or one of the other larger cities and never came to our small town. Since many people did not have the wherewithal to make the trip, particularly since it would probably mean staying overnight, we decided we could bring the artists to them. Norma Helena returned for two concerts, followed by Carlos and Luis Godoy, two brothers who have been writing and performing Nicaraguan music for years. We were sold out every time. After one of her concerts, Norma Helena stayed over and sang for our *ancianos* the following Monday. They were thrilled!

Visitors continued to express interest in the Foundation. Many of them either made a contribution or decided to sponsor a student. It seemed to make sense to see if we couldn't match up each of our students with his/her own sponsor, believing that they would have a more reliable source of support. We never wanted to have to tell a student in mid-course that we could no longer help. That would have meant they would have to quit school and likely not be able to return. We were successful in setting it up, and ever since we have linked sponsor and student. We encourage communication between them, and whenever a sponsor is visiting, do our best to arrange a time for them to meet.

Several of our students have graduated from university and we are very proud of them. One, in fact, is now the president of the local chapter of the PLC political party.

Up to now, we had not done anything with our reserve. We had been advised to let whatever was there grow up for a few years so that we would be better able to see what we had. The area had been lumbered more than once, so there were few really big trees. I collected seeds and like Johnny Appleseed, scattered them all over. I don't think any of them germinated, but perhaps the birds were appreciative.

Finally we decided to clear out the "trash trees" and do some planting of more desirable varieties. Our gardeners, supplemented by others, did the clearing and then dug holes for the new little trees. We had hired a young woman from the States, a landscape architect, to advise us about plantings for the hotel so she supervised the project. Our Foundation students spent a week of their spring vacation planting the 2,500 trees that had been donated to us. Needless to say, they got hot and dirty but seemed to enjoy their work. One thing that is characteristic about Nicaraguans is that they always seem to enjoy whatever they are doing. They laugh, tease each other, and sometimes sing…even construction workers.

We had many discussions about whether we should set up some kind of irrigation system for the new little trees, at least the first year, but some of us, including me, felt they would have to make it on their own. It was the start of the rainy season so we let Mother Nature do her magic and many survived. They are now good-sized trees.

At last the time came to begin work on my house. Originally I had chosen a piece of property near the restaurant/bar, but Chris worried that the noise would bother me and persuaded me to choose another location. There was another area east of the restaurant and south of the first hotel rooms that had always been a favorite spot of mine, so that is where we decided to build. It was to be built into the side of a hill, so Axel and I had many discussions about the design and the special things that I wanted to have incorporated into it. Chris wanted me to follow the design of the other houses that had been built, and there were some features we incorporated, but there were a few things I did not like and did not want.

The design we agreed on was a two-level structure with two bedrooms and a bath on the lower level and the kitchen and living space on the upper level to take advantage of the view. I was persuaded by George to put in a full bathroom on the second level, because as he said "You are growing older and one day you are not going to want to go up and down those stairs." We took his advice.

The stairs ended up being built outside because due to the design of the house, had they been inside they would have been very steep. Fortunately, with this kind of climate, outside is not a problem. The best feature of my house was the large porch to be built over the bedrooms that would afford a wonderful view of the ocean. The target date for completion was Christmas 2004.

Jean's house

Unbeknownst to me, Chris was planning a surprise for me. He had communicated with all my kids, asking them to come to San Juan to help celebrate the completion of my house. Timing was a little tricky because as usual, there were delays. Christmas came and went, but by February the lower level was ready, so I decided to go ahead and move in.

The very day that I moved, Chris summoned me to check out a guest who had fallen. It was not an unusual request because at that time I was the only trained medical person on site and was called on from time to time to check a guest who was not feeling well or who had a fall or similar minor accident. However, this time it seemed strange to me because he headed towards the restaurant and was in such a hurry that I could not keep up with him to ask for details. Later he told me that he had done that because he was tired of telling me lies.

When I entered the restaurant, there seated at a table were my kids! I couldn't believe my eyes! What a wonderful surprise! Not all of them could make it but the biggest surprise was that Ron's wife, Laura, came (and has many times since), as did my daughter Mary, who had told me she would never leave the U.S.

Diane, Dave, and my 3-year-old granddaughter were also part of the group, but of course, they had visited two years earlier. It was a wonderful housewarming present, even though only part of the house was completed.

It took another two months for the upper level to be completed. It is a great pleasure to have my own place. The porch turned out just as I expected. Not only does it offer a wonderful view of the ocean, it has the feeling of a tree house since it is at the height of many of the treetops. It's a joy to watch the birds settling in the trees at dusk and to watch the beautiful sunsets almost every evening.

Since I had my own kitchen again, I needed to shop for food from time to time. Here that is not as simple as jumping in the car and going to the supermarket. We have well-stocked supermarkets, but until just recently, they were all in Managua, a 2½ hour drive. And I don't drive in Nicaragua anymore!

Mercado

However, we do have a local *mercado* or fruit /vegetable market in town, and I shop there several times a week. Their produce is fresh and all locally grown. Since I have gotten to know a number of people in town, it's fun to visit with friends at the same time. Small towns are great! Items other than produce can often be found at one of the many *pulperias* (variety stores). I do make occasional trips to

Managua to stock up on things that are not available in San Juan.

I also have had the benefit of the services of the hotel – the housekeepers clean my house, the gardeners tend my garden, and I can eat in the restaurant whenever I wish. Even my laundry and ironing are taken care of. I could get away with doing nothing if I so chose. What a tough life!

One of the areas of the hotel that had not had a lot of attention was the laundry. I was an advocate for both the housekeepers and laundresses so kept pushing Chris to find a way to improve the laundry facilities. The laundry did not seem to rate high on Chris' list of priorities, but I knew that it would be a vital part of our operation. The women were valiantly trying to keep up with the mountain of sheets and towels from the hotel and tablecloths and napkins from the restaurant. They were using the machines that we had been using for our household and personal laundry and they were getting far behind, even doing some of the work by hand.

Finally Chris realized that something had to be done and ordered commercial machines, which once the women figured out how to use (computer-operated, of course), pretty well took care of the problem. Now the demand has grown so much that a new laundry facility has been built.

14

The end of 2004 arrived with another rush – to finish four houses. Chris had been promised that construction would be complete by November 15th. As usual it wasn't and it looked nip and tuck to have them ready for their owners who were expecting to stay in them over Christmas. We were all frantic, particularly Chris. I had begun work on bedspreads fairly early because I planned to go to Managua to spend Christmas Eve with Maggie, as was our custom. Ever since we had moved to Nicaragua we had only missed one Christmas Eve together.

I had completed 18 bedspreads in all, an assortment of single, queen, and king sizes. I had tried to persuade Chris to have all queen size beds, knowing that the housekeepers would be confused by the different sizes, but he was determined that every master bedroom have a king. Throw pillows also had to be made for the beds from the same fabric as the spreads. Fortunately I had met a local, excellent seamstress who agreed to make them. There were curtains to make as well so I asked Lilliam and her daughter to help me. I took the measurements for the windows in one of the houses, expecting they would all be alike because they were the same floor plan. I went off to Managua thinking my part of the preparations was in good hands.

Maggie and I had our usual pleasant time, visiting our friend Grant, going to mass followed by a reception at the house of several Catholic Sisters who were friends of Maggie's. Maggie and I were friends well before we came to Nicaragua, and as I explained earlier, she was the major reason I chose to come here. Even though she lived in Managua and I in San Juan, we got together several times a month for a few days and often took short trips together. We are near the same age, which was a help to me since I lived with relatively young people the rest of the time. Interests and tastes do seem to vary with different generations. Maggie is a Sister of Charity, and I was raised a Protestant, but we shared many of the same beliefs, were of the same political persuasion, and were very dedicated to the people of Central America, each in our own way. When things got hectic with our project and I was feeling discouraged or depressed I was always able to unburden myself on Maggie. She did the same with me.

Unfortunately Maggie's health was failing. She suffered a bout of cancer (lymphoma), and then fell and broke a hip requiring a replacement operation. A tia (transient ischemic attack or minor stroke) in early 2007 really frightened her about living here alone, so she spent more and more time at her community in Nazareth, Kentucky. Finally in the summer of 2007, she returned to the States for good. It was a great loss for both of us; the end of an era.

When I returned to San Juan Christmas Day, I was met with the news that neither the bedspreads nor the curtains fit. What a blow! I decided not to panic until I could investigate what had happened. As it turned out, the window frames were all different sizes and so the curtains only fit the house that I had measured. It seems that each house, although the same plan, had been built by a different contractor with his own carpenters. As a result the windows were slightly bigger or smaller than my measurements. It required remaking all the curtains but those of the original house. I was really upset and discouraged but Lilliam agreed to help me do the alterations.

The bedspread problem was easier to fix. As I had predicted, the housekeepers who made up the beds did not know that they were all different sizes. They tried to put queen-size on king, single on queen, etc., and could not manage to get them to fit. No surprise there! Once we got them on the right beds, they were fine.

After this experience, the stress it caused, and the fact that we had found competent seamstresses here in town, I told Chris I was resigning from the job of official seamstress. He tried to dissuade me by reassuring me it would not happen again, but I knew better.

In the spring of 2005, my St. Louis friend Nancy Paul came for a visit. On a prior visit she had been impressed by our uniform project. As a result she had applied to her local Rotary Club for a grant of $3,500 to support our work. When you receive a grant from International Rotary you must work with a local Rotary Club which receives the money, then disperses it to the recipient. Our closest club was in Jinotepe, a town about a 1½ hour drive from here. While Nancy was here we attended one of their meetings and met many of the members. After the meeting they treated us to a delicious meal, giving us time to socialize and get better acquainted. We left feeling that they would be happy to work with us on the grant.

We also visited a school where the students were being measured for uniforms. While there Nancy asked the children to make drawings on the squares of material she had brought with her. Her plan was to make the squares into a quilt, which on her next trip would be returned to the school. The children greeted the project with great enthusiasm!

Samuel Church, which I had attended for 20 years when I lived in St. Louis, was celebrating their 100th anniversary that same year. As a part of the celebration the church leaders were asking members to pledge donations to a campaign fund that would be distributed to selected charities. My friend Carolyn suggested to the planning committee that our Foundation be one of the recipients. I was well known by many members of the committee, so Carolyn was confident that we would be chosen.

It seemed prudent to make a trip to St. Louis to express our appreciation to the members of both the church and Rotary Club and to make a presentation about our work to them and any others that might be interested. Lilliam willingly agreed to accompany me. Carolyn invited us to stay with her. Cesar Paniamogan, a superb photographer who lived in San Juan, is also skillful at creating marketing materials, such as pamphlets and posters and doing layouts for newsletters, so he helped us put together a very professional PowerPoint presentation.

Cesar and his partner Dan Polley had retired in San Juan several years earlier. They had first come to Nicaragua in 1995 with Dr. David Belt, the pastor of their church in Kansas City and a group of other members. They visited Mulukuku, a small community in the north part of the country where a North American nurse, Dorothy Granada, had established a health clinic to serve the area. They were so impressed with her work and the people she was serving that they returned every year thereafter with a medical mission led by Dr. Greg Houston, a dental professor and friend. He brought senior dental students to clean and repair the teeth of people in the *campo*, some of whom had never seen a dentist. Dan and Cesar served as volunteers. Like so many of us, they fell in love with the people and beauty of Nicaragua and decided to "retire" here. Dan is also a very excellent photographer and both he and Cesar found their days filled with requests for their work.

While in the States Lilliam and I met with various groups to solicit support for our project. Lilliam does not speak English and although I could translate fairly well in a relaxed social setting I was not capable of doing it for a presentation to more formal groups. Fortunately I have a good friend in St. Louis, Mary Jane Schutzius, who had lived in Bolivia for ten years and is fluent in Spanish. She agreed to translate Lilliam's remarks for our English-speaking audiences. During the first presentation at Samuel Church when Lilliam paused for the translation there was dead silence. When Mary Jane finally realized we were waiting for her, she laughed and said she was so caught up in what Lilliam was saying that she forgot for a moment that she was there to do more than listen. Everyone we spoke to seemed interested in our work and gave us generous donations. When we made our presentation to the Rotary Club we were delighted to hear that we had been awarded the grant Nancy had applied for.

While I was in St. Louis, my daughter, Mary, decided rather precipitously to marry her long-time boyfriend. There was not time to allow other immediate family members to travel, so I was the only one in attendance. They were married in their church. The congregation was invited and many came. Mary had little money and had suggested a reception in her apartment with chicken wings and pizza, but my two friends, Marcia and Mary, would not hear of that and offered to cater the event. Marcia is a gourmet cook, so the food was very special – a far cry from what Mary had planned. Carolyn supplied the cake, and I provided sparkling cider. Her dad sent her money for flowers, so all in all, it was a very nice occasion and they both were very pleased.

Later that year Maggie and I made our last trip of many we had made together in Nicaragua. It was to the Soletiname islands at the south end of Lake Nicaragua. These are a group of more than 30 islands, the larger ones inhabited by small numbers of people. They have earned a reputation over the years for being an artists' colony.

Maggie Fisher

The Soletiname islands also played an important role in the revolution of 1979. Ernesto Cardenal, a renowned priest, had formed a group of the residents to study the Gospels from a *campesino* perspective. The dictator, Anastasio Somoza, saw this as a center for dissent, a little pocket of independence in the midst of repression which might provide hope for others. He sent his *guardia*, his personal police force, to squelch the community. The *campesinos* fought back valiantly, but were outnumbered and did not have the armaments to counter those of the *guardia*. However, this was one of the first of many uprisings that succeeded in finally overthrowing the dictator.

We visited the historic sight and talked about the experience with some of the widows, who were still living there. Even after close to 30 years it was still very vivid in their minds.

Dan and Cesar accompanied us and discovered the area was a photographer's paradise. We travelled down the Papaturra River and saw all kinds of wildlife and birds. The captain was unable to use the motor because of the amount of vegetation in the river, so used a pole to push the boat along. Actually that enhanced the trip because without the motor noise we didn't frighten the wildlife as much and were able to hear the sounds of the forest much more clearly. Dan and Cesar had ample time to take many excellent photos. Maggie said it was just like being on the African Queen as the foliage was very jungle-like and frequently brushed up against the sides of the boat. Sadly, there was no Humphrey Bogart!

A memorable event was our engine conking out in the middle of Lake Nicaragua when we were on the way back to the hotel. I think probably some of the vegetation we travelled through had gotten tangled in the boat's propellers. We were in sight of our hotel but it took some time for anyone to see us and come to the rescue.

Fortunately our guide, who was also the hotel owner, had brought along some watermelon so we were able to enjoy refreshments while we waited.

As this hotel was on one of the islands they had to bring all their supplies in by boat twice a week from the mainland. This included their ice supply. They had electricity provided by solar power and a generator but, as it was somewhat limited, it was used for more important purposes such as lights, fans, and refrigeration. Unlike us North Americans, Nicaraguans don't use a lot of ice. In the evenings the four of us would have drinks while we watched the sun set over the lake. We would use up their ice supply for the week in one sitting! All in all, we had a great experience, our only complaint being that the menu did not vary from day to day. Since there were no other restaurants on the island we ate all our meals at the hotel. There was always plenty and the quality was very good which made up for the lack of variety.

Many people come to Nicaragua and expect the food to be like that of Mexico. It's quite different. Beans, rice, and tortillas, along with plantain and corn are the mainstays of the diet but none are prepared to be spicy, or *picante* as they say here. The most common restaurant meal is a salad of shredded cabbage topped with carrot, beet, and cucumber slices followed with a serving of chicken, fish, pork, or beef with french fries and rice. Yes, both. Most of the food is fried. Because San Juan is so close to the ocean, lobster, shrimp, and fresh fish are almost always available and very reasonable.

There is a restaurant in Managua that serves traditional food and the selection is much larger and tastier. It is called Doña Haydee, the name of the founder. One time when I was visiting my son in California, his wife wanted to make a Nicaraguan dish called Indio Viejo that she had enjoyed at Doña Haydee's in Managua. While visiting San Juan several months earlier, she had asked some of the women who worked for us for a recipe and had bought a few ingredients at the *mercado* that were not readily available in Irvine. Since the recipe was handwritten it was not very legible, so Ron decided to check Doña Haydee's web site for her recipe. Of course, the directions were in Spanish, so he tried out his translator on the computer. Have you ever used one? If not, you will find it quite hilarious, or at least we did. One of the ingredients was lard (yes, they still use it here) and it was translated as "butter of the pig." That gave us quite a laugh.

Unfortunately it is not just the computer translator that is amusing. Many times we have looked at a pamphlet that has been written in Spanish and translated into English with a dictionary in hand, or so it appears. One that particularly amused me was promoting the nursing school of a local university. There was a picture of several young nurses with their right hand in the air saying the Florence Nightingale "bad word," the translation for "oath." I wonder how my nursing school would have felt about that! I don't want to infer that translation into Spanish from English is perfect. I'm sure it causes as many laughs as the reverse.

15

As time went on, Chris continued to purchase land and build more houses. I was becoming more uncomfortable all the time about the direction our project was taking. I seemed to know less and less about what was going on. When I first came to San Juan we shared a house, and each evening we would sit on the porch with a beer and talk about the day's activities and what was planned for the coming days and weeks. Once we moved to the hotel property, we continued the practice for some months but often we had guests and could not discuss business.

The office had been in the house where we originally lived and I was very aware of what was happening, sometimes too much so! Not any more. It was in a separate building (Sandra and John's house). There were increasing demands on Chris' time, so he had less time to just sit leisurely and talk about what was being planned. Decisions were being made that I would hear about second or third hand. When Chris and I discussed this, he said he didn't want me to worry and besides he felt I might not approve of his decisions…and often times he was right.

I never had any idea of being a developer. It seemed to me that was what we were becoming. When I expressed my concerns to George (who was now supervising construction and materials), he told me that if we didn't develop the land someone else would, and we could do it better. Judging by what had been built already that was certainly true, but I just could not overcome my uneasiness with the direction we were taking. So as not to be a drag on everyone else's enthusiasm, I finally came to the conclusion that my best course would be to distance myself from the project and devote my time and energies to the Foundation. After all the years of working and planning together it was a hard decision to make and upset Chris a great deal, but it seemed the only solution to me.

As more and more guests visited our hotel, they were impressed by the help the Foundation was providing the young people of our town. Often visitors were looking for a way to help Nicaraguans and the Foundation provided the perfect vehicle. Since Chris and I lived on site and were able to supervise the distribution of the money, people felt more secure about their donations. Another feature that made our program attractive was that we had no administration costs – they were paid by PEPO (the hotel), so all the donated money went directly to students or programs.

People buying houses on our property for investment purposes often chose our development over others because of the work of the Foundation. Many even decided to sponsor a student. We received many donations from investors and hotel guests which allowed us to provide additional uniforms and increase the number of scholarship students. We were delighted that we could help so many more young people.

"This area is being kept clean by Students United Against Litter"

Our community service projects continued and expanded. The numbers of older adults attending our *ancianos* meeting each month continued to increase, and our litter pick-up became confined to a specific part of town that we had chosen to keep clean. I asked for a volunteer among the students to make us a sign to indicate what we were doing. German, the one who volunteered, was a student in law school and a self-taught artist as well. I had expected a small sign, the kind I was accustomed to seeing in the States, but I should have known better. German painted a large beautiful sign and we erected it in a prominent spot in the area. Unfortunately signs tend to get defaced. I was worried that this work of art might suffer the same fate, and it has.

My son John and his family came in the summer of 2005 for a two-week visit. His wife had never been outside the U.S. before and was very nervous about the cultural differences that she would encounter here. John, however, had spent ten days after his college graduation in the Dominican Republic, so he had a good feel for what he might experience in Nicaragua. Their children, Rachel (10) and Gwen (3) seemed to feel they were just in a different part of the U.S., albeit a strange one. Gwen was a very active child and needed a lot of close supervision. She loved the local people and was content the few times we left her in the care of a babysitter. Rachel was a little more adventuresome but her parents curtailed her activities somewhat as they were uncertain of the safety on our property and in the town. Like many parents in the States their fear level had been raised by all the unfortunate publicity that the media continues to promote about child abductions and the like.

Shortly after they arrived, Rachel and I were walking in town and I asked her how she liked San Juan. She said, "It's not what I expected." When I asked what she expected, she said, "Well, there are no malls, there is no

Disneyland, or Lego Land, and it's very annoying because the people always speak to me in Spanish!" Sounds pretty much like a typical American adolescent, doesn't she! I explained that she was in Nicaragua, a very poor country, which could not afford all those places she took for granted in the U.S., and the reason they spoke Spanish to her was because it is the native language here. I'm not sure she understood, but apparently it didn't worry her much. She loves to swim so she enjoyed our pool and the ocean, and she was intrigued by our large variety of animals. We had a great visit, went sightseeing to many places, and I think they left with the feeling they would like to return.

The last of my children to visit was my oldest daughter, Katie and her husband. Arthur was paralyzed for a year after receiving immunizations prior to travel in India back in the 1970s. He has recovered most of his faculties but still has to wear braces on his legs when he walks. Our many steps were a problem for him. Although we offered him transportation whenever he wanted it, he seemed pretty content to stay at the house, reading, watching TV, or sitting on the porch enjoying the beautiful view and the activities of the town. The pool was close enough that he could enjoy the sun and the water.

Katie, on the other hand, explored San Juan from top to bottom. She loved going to the market, buying tortillas from the tortilla lady, talking with the locals, and exploring the rocky coastline on the north side of the bay. She and Arthur were welcome to eat in the restaurant, but preferred to eat Nicaraguan food, so we arranged with the women in the kitchen to prepare their food each day. It pleased everyone – those who ate and those who cooked. I think it was an unusual circumstance for the women that a pair of gringos would prefer their food to that of our restaurant, and they loved it!

A few months later the Shatagin family was visiting the hotel. The family members were Betsy, her daughter Kim and her son-in-law John. They had established a foundation in the U.S. in memory of Betsy's son and Kim's brother, Christopher, who died at an early age. He had been a passionate baseball fan, so they had created the foundation to raise money to support baseball camps for boys and girls in the inner cities in their area.

They were very interested in our Foundation and as we talked about how we might work together, I said that as far as I knew there had never been a baseball camp in San Juan. Since baseball is very popular in Nicaragua I thought the children would love it. They offered to purchase enough bats, balls, gloves, and shirts for 24 youngsters and arrange to have them sent to us. They even included money to pay for a coach. The camp would be held for two weeks in July during the school break. Children ages 8-10 would be recruited.

An older man had taught many of the young people in town to play over the years, so he seemed a perfect choice for coach. Unfortunately, he had his own agenda so the camp did not go as planned. We thought he had understood the concept, but apparently not. The equipment was bought for young children and was too small for the older boys that he recruited. It was clear it was the coach's idea to create a team, not direct a camp.

However, that did not deter either the Shatagins or us from trying again. We found two other young men to coach the next one and they did a great job. It is so enjoyable to watch the children practice and remember back to when my children were that age. They make the same mistakes – overthrowing the bases, dropping the ball, getting distracted out in the outfield and watching the ball go between their legs. That doesn't interfere with their enthusiasm one bit! Girls as well as boys are recruited, and their skill level is equivalent. We continue to hold two camps each year rotating primary schools, so many more children have an opportunity to learn.

16

Over the years we have tried various ways to raise money for the Foundation. Almost all our donations are directed toward our uniform or scholarship projects, so usually do not include extra to cover the community service programs. The students wished to help and held a *feria* (craft fair) one December and at several holiday times they set up a booth in the park to sell food to the locals. Although on the whole they did well, and I appreciated them wanting to make the effort, it was more work than benefit. I remembered church bazaars all too well!

I mentioned the concerts that we held to attract local people to our hotel, and in that regard they were successful but as a money-raising effort they were not. By the time we paid the artists and associated costs there wasn't much left over. One year we tried offering ethnic dinners from different countries of the world and although they were well attended, the costs of the unusual food that our chef prepared ate up the proceeds. Our most recent effort has been calendars featuring pictures taken in San Juan by Dan and Cesar, and designed by Cesar. Since they volunteered their time and efforts, our only cost was the printing. The calendars have been very popular and we plan to continue to offer them every year.

Nicaraguans love parties and celebrations. The local Roman Catholic Church celebrates various saints' days throughout the year. These are punctuated by setting off rockets and by music performed by the local band. I thought once my kids were grown I would never have to listen to junior high school level music again, but I was wrong! At least they play with enthusiasm and their singing matches it in volume…and dissonance.

Twice a year there are special celebrations. At the end of June there is a two-day holiday to commemorate the patron saint of San Juan, St John the Baptist and in September, all of Central America celebrates Independence Day. For this occasion young people dress up in traditional garb and parade around town to the beat of drums and whirling batons. There are speeches, entertainment, and fireworks. Those more adventuresome souls participate in climbing a greased pole, chasing a greased pig, and bull baiting in the local arena. It's an event for young and old to enjoy.

Birthdays are particularly important here and are celebrated by young and old. Chris' birthday is October 1st and mine is the 2nd so we always shared the celebration.

Each year Chris vowed that we would leave town to avoid the parties but something always came up and we never left. He claimed to hate the parties, but I suspect would have been disappointed if they didn't occur. The Foundation students usually surprise me with a party, but now that it happens every year it is no longer a surprise. However I am appreciative and always enjoy it. Presents are an important part of the celebration and Nicaraguans love *adornos* (knick knacks). Since I have been trying very hard to not accumulate sit-arounds (so named by my friend, Gloria) I end up contributing most of them to our *ancianos* as bingo prizes.

One year when Chris was vehement that he didn't want a party, I suggested that we have a cake, serve it in the restaurant, and invite everyone to come wish him happy birthday and enjoy a piece of cake. That created all kinds of dissension among our staff, particularly the kitchen help, and we were told, in no uncertain terms, that was NOT the way to celebrate a birthday. It's not a party without traditional food, lots to drink and, of course, dancing.

One birthday custom we enjoy here is being wakened early in the morning or late at night with a mariachi band performing favorite latino songs including "Las Mañanitas" which is traditional.

Up to now I had not had many visitors from the States, other than family. However my friends Mary and Nev Haggins came in October, 2006, for a two-week visit. Actually they are from Canada. Mary and I have known each other since we were in grade school. We had a lot of fun reminiscing about friends we had both known as kids. Mary remembered many more than I, but then she stayed in the same community or close to it and was able to keep in touch. I, on the other hand, left Canada when I was in high school and was so busy making new friends that I lost contact with many of the friends I had known earlier.

While they were here, we went to visit the volcano at Masaya which is still active, and were assailed by noxious fumes that drove us immediately back to the car. I had visited this volcano many times, but never experienced before the intensity of the fumes of that day. We were all coughing and it took some time for our lungs to stop hurting.

When we were returning to San Juan, our driver passed a stopped school bus. Mary asked if there was not a law against that in Nicaragua. I laughed and explained that it was not a school bus here, but a regular one. We always say that Central America is where school buses come to die.

Our *ancianos* group had grown so large that we were having trouble transporting them to and from our gatherings. Our practice was to bring the participants to the restaurant in taxis, but since only four or five could be carried at one time, it took many trips and a lot of time to bring them and deliver them back to their homes. Some of the students came up with the idea to buy a bus. The big drawback was that we did not have the money to buy a new one. Buying used vehicles is risky anywhere but especially in Nicaragua where, due to financial constraints, maintenance is not a priority.

There was a family from the U.S. who had been very generous to us and to different projects in town, and we decided to see how open they would be to helping us. Chris had suggested that PEPO could put up the money for half of a new bus if we would agree to allow PEPO to use it when there were large groups of hotel guests to transport. They would also handle upkeep and maintenance and provide a driver when needed. This seemed like a perfect deal for the Foundation so we took him up on the offer. The family agreed to pay the rest.

It took several months to have the bus delivered, but since it is a 21-passenger, it helped replace many of the taxis we had used for the transportation of the old folks. It also allowed the students to take some field trips and facilitated the transportation of large groups of hotel guests. It has been a valuable addition.

We began to look at ways to attract people from town to our reserve. Our goal was not only to preserve green space but, in line with our mission, to provide education to children and adults about their unique ecosystem and to instruct them in ways to help preserve it. This is a dry tropical area which means, among other things, there is a six month dry season and six month rainy season. Plants and animals have to adapt to survive, and we wanted to have exhibits demonstrating how they were able to accomplish this.

A veterinarian had joined our staff, and he had become very active in rescuing animals that had been mistreated or wounded, returning them to the wild whenever possible. However, we had collected a number of them that were not able to survive without our help. We were housing them here on our property. It began to feel like we were competing with the local zoo! His plan was to establish a wildlife area on the reserve where they would be happier and visitors could enjoy them more or less in their native habitat. We had planted trees and built several trails through the reserve along which we intended to place signs indicating the different types of indigenous trees. Chris suggested that we think about building a natural science museum on the reserve grounds that would house educational materials and be a place where teachers could bring school children on field trips. All we needed to do was raise the money to build it. Another challenge!

17

Chris and I met with two young men, originally from Atlanta, who were promoting their new magazine, "El Puente" ("The Bridge"), and were looking for businesses to buy advertising space. We liked what we saw, particularly because it was in both languages and, as its title suggested, was intended to build bridges between the different cultures. The writing was done by Jon Thompson and some Nicaraguan staff. The photos were taken by the other partner, Eric Volz. The articles were primarily about San Juan, and to a certain extent, Nicaragua, and were meant to inform all the residents about local activities, travel opportunities, and national concerns. It was a timely publication because more and more foreigners were investing and building, especially in San Juan and wanted to know more about the town and country they were living in.

Several months after we first met Jon, Genessa, our marketing director at the time, asked to have a meeting with Chris, Jon, and me to discuss the possibility of hiring him to work for the hotel or the Foundation in some capacity. The magazine was not producing enough profit for Jon to support himself and his Nicaraguan wife and he was looking for additional opportunities to supplement his income.

Jon had been coming to San Juan since 1998, had met Arelis, a local young woman, and after several years they decided to marry. Jon was working at that time for United Way in Atlanta. Arelis joined him there for about three years. Since her family lived here and Nicaraguans have very close-knit families, she and Jon decided to come back and settle in San Juan.

We were impressed with Jon, as we had been the first time we met him, and decided to give him a trial, working half-time for PEPO and the other half for the Foundation. We felt his experience at United Way, a non-profit organization, would benefit us. Another advantage for me was that Jon was bilingual, fluent in both English and Spanish, and since very few of our students could speak English, this would be a great plus.

Jon jumped right in and soon became indispensable. Since the Foundation had grown rapidly and was basically a "mom and pop" organization, we were in need of systems to help keep track of data – our finances in particular. Arlen kept good records but they were not in a form easy to access. We were behind on some of our donations and needed a tracking method for alerting us when a donor was delinquent. Most of our donations came to our treasurer in Boston, and since we received notice by mail that a payment had been made there was a time lag before we knew about it. This added to the difficulty of staying on top of things. Jon worked hard to help us get our data in good order and easily accessible. He arranged with our treasurer in Boston to allow us to access the bank records there so that we could check donations frequently. It ruffled a few feathers in the office, but on the whole was greeted with cooperation.

Fundacion A. Jean Brugger staff: Veronica, Jean, Jon, and Arlen

By this time our staff had expanded to include one of our students, Veronica, on a part-time basis. Her main function, besides filing and assisting Arlen, was to interact with the myriad of people who came to us for help with problems, such as sick children needing medicine, etc. Chris and I had established a fund, which I called the Good Samaritan Fund, for this purpose. We each contributed to it monthly. It was really done in self-defense because we were continually being petitioned for help. This way we could refer people to Veronica. She could evaluate their needs better than Chris or I.

One of our students, Sandra, was about to graduate in systems engineering from Upoli, our local university. Jobs are not readily available in San Juan in particular, but also throughout Nicaragua. She and a classmate had a plan to establish an Internet café in Tola, a small community near Rivas, the largest town in the area. The development of the beaches near Tola brought an influx of foreigners into the community. At the time there was no way for the new residents to access the Internet except by going to Rivas, 20–30 minutes away. The young women put a business plan together, found a location, and hoped I might be able to help them find financial backing.

Karen, Sandra's classmate and business partner (hopefully), was also graduating from Upoli, but had a chronic debilitating disease that left her with the use of only her right arm. Her fellow students used to carry her from class to class as she had no wheelchair, at school or at home. At home, once Karen was dressed and seated in a chair, she was there until someone came along to move her, as her mother, a schoolteacher, was gone during the day. Fortunately she had family living nearby.

I wasn't sure I could find backing for their business, but I thought I might be able to find someone to donate a wheelchair. Since she had only the use of her right hand and arm, a conventional wheelchair would not be helpful when she was by herself.

We approached several people in the States. Very fortunately Chris thought of a dentist who had recently bought a house site on our property. Since he is a paraplegic and confined to a wheelchair, he was eager to help someone with a like need. He had an associate whose grandmother had been confined to an electric wheelchair before she died. Since her family no longer had use for the chair, they were very happy to donate it to Karen. When Dr. Williams came to San Juan a couple of months later, he brought the wheelchair with him.

He and his parents went with us to Karen's home to deliver the chair. Her whole family was there to greet us. Karen was thrilled and appreciative of all our efforts. She would now be mobile and relatively independent, a whole new experience. For us, just to see the smile on her face said it all.

When you work with young people you have to expect weddings and babies. Our first wedding was Arlen's who married her long-time sweetheart, Joel, in October of 2005. Her brother, Vladimir, followed in December and there have been several others since.

Weddings here are very similar to what we experience in the States. Often the bride wears a traditional wedding dress and has several attendants, particularly if it's a church wedding. However, weddings also take place in homes, hotels like ours, and on the beach. There may or may not be a religious ceremony, but there is always a civil ceremony conducted by a judge. And, as is typical of all celebrations, there is a lot of food and drink and, of course, music and dancing.

Very soon the babies started arriving so we have already begun to prepare the second generation for the Foundation. Since extended families live together, having a baby doesn't have to interfere with work or school. While mama is away someone else in the household steps in to take over the care of the child – sometimes the grandmother, or an aunt, or even a great-grandmother.

I had begun to think seriously about retiring from the everyday work of the Foundation. I was approaching my 75th birthday and was finding that the Foundation was taking up more and more of my time and energy. It seemed there was less time for the things I wanted to do, even things as simple as getting my hair cut or shopping for fruit and vegetables in the market. I didn't want my age and energy level to hinder the growth and vitality of the Foundation.

When I discussed this with Chris, he was worried that without me the character of the Foundation would change and that I would have less and less interaction with others. I assured him that I would still take an active role in guiding the Foundation and had no plans to become a recluse.

As I began seriously to consider who might take over as director, my first thought was Arlen. We had talked for sometime about her future and it was clear she was dedicated to the Foundation and planned to remain working for it unless something unexpected interfered. She is also Nicaraguan. My goal had long been for a Nicaraguan to eventually take over as director.

The big drawbacks for Arlen were that she was pregnant with her first child, lacked fluency in English, and had not completed her college courses. Most of our donors are English-speaking and communication with them has to be in English. Arlen had been studying English, but the pregnancy interfered, and she quit without reaching the point of being comfortable in speaking it to others. I felt she was not ready to take on the job of director, but knew she had been counting on it, so it was not going to be easy to tell her.

18

In June of 2006 I realized ten years had passed since Chris, Leslie, and I had formed our partnership. It didn't seem possible. Where had the time gone! I decided it merited a celebration and Chris concurred. I had taken many snapshots of our progress over the years and I talked with Cesar about how we might display them to share with others. He suggested we select the most informative ones and he would transfer them to his computer to make a PowerPoint presentation. We felt it would be helpful to include a chronology of events to go with the pictures. I had started journaling before coming to Nicaragua and had continued the practice, so it meant reviewing all my old journals to establish important events and dates. It was fun to go back and read about all our concerns about delays and money that had receded into the background once the hotel was open and doing well.

I invited as many of the original players as were in town and we had a lot of fun looking at the pictures and reminiscing about the various steps and detours we had taken over the years. We have had opportunities to share the presentation with others since. Invariably people who are familiar with how the hotel looks now are fascinated to see how it looked when the site was in its original state and during construction phases.

I continued to consider who might take over the Foundation, and it occurred to me that perhaps Jon would be willing to be an interim director until Arlen was ready. When I approached him about it, he was pleased, but wanted to talk with his wife before he made a decision. A few days later, Jon met with me and told me he would be happy to take on the job. Now my task was to explain to Arlen what was happening. Needless to say, she was disappointed and somewhat hurt, but could see the reasoning behind it. She and I had become quite close over the years of working together and we were both a little sad to see that end. We agreed that Jon would spend the month of December learning the ropes, although he was quite familiar with all the aspects of the Foundation by then.

On January 1, 2007, I retired from active involvement in the day to day routine of the Foundation. Jon and I continue to meet regularly for him to apprise me of the current activities and to seek advice and counsel about future directions. Our relationship is such that I am free to make suggestions and share ideas without him feeling threatened.

2006 was a year for celebration. Besides the ten-year anniversary party, we celebrated my oldest son's 50th birthday in California. All the family members could attend plus Mark, Ron's boyhood friend, and his wife. We had a joyful time together. I feel very fortunate that my kids seem more my friends than my children, and I think they consider me a friend as well. One of the highlights of that particular visit was having dinner with my two boys at a Japanese restaurant halfway between their homes. Normally when we are together, there are wives and children around all vying for attention. This was a rare opportunity for me to have their undivided attention, and I treasured it.

In September we received the news that Axel, our former construction boss, had committed suicide. We were devastated. Like always in those cases, we wondered why, and whether we could we have done something to prevent it. He had resigned from his position with us about a year before, informing Chris that he wanted a change and new challenges. We were sad to see him go because he had been with us from the beginning and was one of the PEPO family. I was particularly affected because Axel had played such an important part in building my house and the waterfall next to it. I suggested we dedicate the waterfall to his memory. We subsequently did, installing a plaque with his name next to it and holding a little ceremony in his honor. The friends who attended were very appreciative of an opportunity to share memories and say farewell.

The other very tragic event we experienced that year was the death of our good friend, Luis. Luis was another person who was part of the family. Chris had known him for more than fifteen years, and I had known him since I arrived in San Juan. He was our purchasing agent in Managua because he knew the city so well and made friends with all the vendors with whom we dealt, which usually facilitated our business transactions. Whenever we needed something, we consulted Luis as to where to find it. There were no super stores in Managua so there was no way you could do one-stop shopping. He was always anxious to meet my family members and since his own mother died of cancer when he was fairly young, he considered me his substitute mother.

Luis had health problems for many years, and I must admit we had gotten rather blasé about it. He was always going on some diet or trying out some new fad. We felt that was the reason for his health problems. He began to lose weight, which at first seemed to suit him. He was proud of his new image, but as time went on the weight loss just didn't stop. He had an operation from which he was not able to recuperate. He continued to feel pain and couldn't seem to fend off the complicating infections. His health deteriorated rapidly and he was hospitalized for several days, at which time he was diagnosed with AIDS. His doctors tried the new medications, which we were hopeful would help him recover, but it was not to be. He died peacefully here in my house with us all around him.

He is still missed. Every time we go to Managua we think of Luis, and remember his lively spirit and his vast knowledge of the city. He had requested that his ashes be thrown into the Masaya volcano and so we, his family, and many friends were present to say goodbye. Traditional funerals in Nicaragua are much more personal than those of North Americans. Actually, they are probably similar to what was the practice in the States before the funeral industry began. There normally is no embalming. The family prepares the body for burial. After some type of religious service the casket is transported in the back of a pick-up to the cemetery. Family and friends follow on foot. After a short service at the graveside, the casket is opened and the mourners crowd around for one last look and touch. I have attended several funerals and am always touched by the expressions of love and caring that are such an integral part of the ceremony.

19

With the advent of 2007, a new era began for me. I had relinquished my position as director of the Foundation. For a few days I felt kind of lost. It had been my practice to spend most of my mornings in the office, arriving there about 9 AM. Now I no longer had to do that. I could have a leisurely breakfast, enjoy several cups of coffee, read or just enjoy sitting on my porch listening to the birds. It was a very liberating experience. I must admit I felt left out sometimes when events were being planned that I had had no hand in, but it was also nice not to have to worry if, or how, they were going to be done. I could even attend the *ancianos* meetings like any other *anciano* and be fed and entertained with no effort on my part. I had left the Foundation in very capable hands.

In January my good friend Grant Gallup celebrated his 75th birthday. As mentioned earlier, Maggie and I had lived with Grant when we first came to Nicaragua. Since I had celebrated my 75th the October previously, Maggie decided to plan a celebration for the two of us. She invited many mutual friends from Managua, and, of course, our friends from San Juan. Many nice tributes were made to both of us. I kidded Grant that I had never been allowed to celebrate my birthday alone since I came to Nicaragua; usually it was with Chris but this time it was with him.

Jean and Grant Gallup

Chris finally found an assistant that he could trust and began experimenting with some short trips away from PEPO. His first was to Costa Rica for a week-end with some friends and wouldn't you know, while he was gone, a fire started in one of the houses. It was quite a job to put it out. There was no road access to the burning house; even when the fire truck arrived (from Rivas!) they could not get very close. It is also a very tall house and the fire was in the roof and upper levels, so the bucket brigade our staff set up did not do a lot of good.

We were fortunate to have a fireman from the States staying in the hotel at the time, and he helped coordinate the efforts. Finally they decided to use our power washer that is used to clean the algae off our brick walkways. It was able to direct water to the roof where the flames were the worst. Besides all of our staff being on hand, many people from town came to see how they could help. It took some time, but they were finally able to get it under control.

Sadly, it was not our first fire. We had feared fire from the outset because of our thatched rancho and the fact that a lot of wood was used in constructing our houses. Nicaraguan houses are particularly vulnerable to fire because many still use wood for cooking and their houses are often made of flimsy materials.

Our first fire had occurred several years before in the *bodega* (warehouse) where we stored materials, including adobe and straw bale, plus some furniture and mementoes. It was not located on our property, but was close enough that I was worried a stray spark might ignite our rancho roof. I asked one of our gardeners to keep hosing it down. When the fire was detected people came running with hoses and buckets and did their best until the fire engine came. Because of the fear that it would spread to the houses nearby, people were moving belongings out of their houses to where they hoped they would be safe. Of particular concern was a nearby warehouse where many people stored belongings. It was also being emptied. Fortunately neither it nor nearby houses were damaged.

When at last the *bodega* fire was out, there was very little left that could be salvaged, so it was quite a loss for us. Some people felt the straw had spontaneously combusted and started the fire, but later it was reported that a nearby electric wire was being rubbed against the roof by the wind and was throwing off sparks.

It was a new experience for me to see how people cope with that kind of emergency without the backup we are so used to. Everyone is willing to do what they can to help. With the house, fortunately the contents were not damaged except for the wooden cabinets in the upper story, and, of course, the roof had to be replaced. At first Chris said he could never leave again, but once he evaluated the situation, it was clear that there was nothing he could have done to prevent it, nor could he have done a better job of mobilizing the staff. He subsequently made two more trips to the States that year.

Before the hotel opened the original group of us used to gather at sundown for a drink around the pool. It was a way to keep in touch since we often didn't see each other during the day. The group varied in size depending on who was in town at the time. Once the hotel and restaurant opened some of the group was busy taking care of guests and there were more and more people around the pool, so the rest of us gradually stopped coming. We all felt the loss, so I decided to hold a happy hour at my house on Monday evenings at sunset and invite any of the original group who wanted to attend. We have continued the practice and everyone seems to enjoy it a lot. There is always lots of cheese, crackers, and wine. Everyone contributes something – snacks or a bottle of wine. Not everyone comes every time, but usually we have a group of six or more. The conversation varies from politics to gossip and invariably there's a lot of laughter. I find I enjoy playing hostess once again.

In April 2007, I made a trip to the States to take care of my five-year-old granddaughter for two weeks while her parents, Dave and Diane, attended a seminar. My daughter Mary came from St. Louis to share the baby-sitting chores. I had forgotten about five-year-olds and how active they can be, plus this little one has a mind of her own. Needless to say, we butted heads a few times. My son John and his family drove from California to spend a few days with us. Reisha really enjoyed having her cousins visit and Mary and I enjoyed some adult companionship.

When my daughter and her husband returned, we were all glad to see them, especially Reisha. I did enjoy spending time with my granddaughter, especially since it doesn't happen very often, but missed having more time with my daughter, Diane.

A few days after their return, Mary and I travelled to St. Louis. I wanted to take advantage of the trip to update and express our appreciation to the two groups who had supported us previously. The presentations I made were to the Rotary Club of O'Fallon, IL, which had awarded us the grant the year before, and to Samuel Church, which had donated some of its campaign funds to our uniform project. Each pledged to keep helping us in the future, so the trip was worthwhile.

A shop dedicated to teaching scuba diving opened in San Juan. The owner had taught scuba for years and decided he wanted to branch out to include people with disabilities. Immediately I thought of Karen, the young woman to whom we had donated the electric wheelchair. She was open to the idea, so we arranged for her to come to our pool where Glen was teaching a young paralyzed man to dive. The first time she just watched, but then decided to give it a try. I must say she showed incredible courage. Not only were the instructions given in English, a language she did not know, but she had to trust that the instructors would keep her safe. She loved it and would have continued, but transportation got to be a problem as she lived 45 minutes away in Tola.

Unfortunately she missed a trip with the group to Corn Island off the east coast of Nicaragua where the waters of the Caribbean are perfect for diving. I was in the States and unable to help coordinate her trip. I felt badly that I had let her down.

The summer brought a new challenge for the Foundation. A couple from California bought a building in town that they hoped to develop sometime in the future. In the interim they wanted to donate the use of it to the Foundation.

When Jon and I went to see it, we were appalled at the condition it was in. It could not be used without major renovations. We did not have the money for such extensive repairs but the owners, when they heard of our dilemma, agreed to put up the money to make it usable. We had brainstormed several ideas about how we might use it and finally agreed on an art gallery where local artists could display their work. Since our focus is on education, we decided we would like to add art classes in various mediums for everyone, but primarily the children.

There was a lot of enthusiasm for the project, mainly because there was no other place like it in town. A lot of artists wanted to participate. The owners planned a visit for August. Fortunately the rehab work was almost complete, so we planned a reception for them and invited many locals as well as foreigners. It was a great success – the building was clean and attractive and the walls were covered with art. The owners were very pleased and, in fact, agreed to assist us by fundraising among their friends and acquaintances in the States. Several of our Foundation students are taking an active part in facilitating the work of the gallery.

20

December of 2007 marked the four-year anniversary of the hotel opening. Our hotel manager Jiff Cornwell arranged a celebration in the restaurant to commemorate the occasion. Many of our employees attended and Chris and I were toasted with champagne and congratulated by all. Of course we were expected to say a few words. I still find it difficult to speak extemporaneously in Spanish. If I can prepare and practice it's okay, but otherwise I feel like I stumble around and am probably not understood anyway. However, everyone is very generous and seems to know that my words are sincere and from the heart.

We have now completed a ten-year plus odyssey. San Juan del Sur is a much different place than it was when I came. The foreign community has grown incredibly and there are many more restaurants, hotels, and shops. The hills surrounding town are dotted with many new homes, some of them quite luxurious. There is a new sports park and civic center. New administrative offices have been built for the *alcalde* (mayor) and the *alcaldia* (town council). Many of the streets in town have been upgraded and new street lights installed.

Several cruise ship lines visit our port during cruise season, but unfortunately the passengers usually do not stay in our town. They often sign up for tours while still aboard the ship and are met by buses on the dock that transport them to other attractions, such as Masaya or Granada. These cities are both interesting places to visit, but it disappoints the Sanjuaneños who would like to demonstrate their particular form of hospitality.

For example, the first ship that arrived several years ago was met with a band and a parade featuring folk dancers in full costume. Artisans had set up booths displaying their wares, hoping that something would appeal to the tourists as they shopped for souvenirs. They were very disappointed when they discovered that the visitors were going elsewhere.

It's difficult to know how the local people feel about all this "progress," but I know they are thankful for more jobs and more money coming into the community. For those of us who have been here for some time and know the downside of development, we worry that the unique character of San Juan that attracted so many of us will gradually be lost. One other worrisome aspect is that with more wealth in the community there is more crime, which was almost non-existent when I arrived.

My dream of helping young people obtain an education is being fulfilled every day. We provide uniforms so that children can attend primary school and scholarships for high school and university students, but it is still not enough. Since the educational system here is based on learning by rote, creative thinking is not emphasized or even suggested. I think this is a result of the years of oppression that Nicaraguans have experienced, first by Spain, then by the many dictators who have been supported and abetted by the U.S. That kind of governance does not encourage people to think for themselves, and in some cases has ruthlessly suppressed it.

The last few governments, although democratically elected, have not provided sufficient financial support for education. Teachers are not well prepared and supplies are almost non-existent. It amazes me how dedicated so many of them are to the teaching profession. A future direction for the Foundation is to help train teachers so that they can begin to offer the students a much more varied curriculum with opportunities to problem solve. I feel this is a skill that will allow students to acquire higher levels of achievement, both personally and professionally.

In the fall of 2009 I, along with many other people involved with Pelican Eyes, was shocked to learn the hotel was on the verge of bankruptcy and the bank ready to foreclose. Unfortunately for Chris, his unorthodox and sometimes illegal ways of finding money to finance the costs of the hotel caught up with him. Fortunately a group of local and foreign investors made the decision to try to rescue the hotel by taking on the debt with the bank. Chris was asked to step down and a whole new management team took over the operations of the hotel.

There have been many repercussions from Chris' actions but due to the belt-tightening and improved accounting of the new team the hotel is once more doing well and attracting guests. The Foundation has weathered this storm and with the help of many supporters, including our student sponsors and new board members, will continue to serve the educational needs of the community into the foreseeable future.

I feel that the Foundation is in good, capable, caring hands. I still offer guidance, suggestions, and advice to the staff, but leave the day-to-day activities for them to complete. I am content to fill my life with visiting family, reading, listening to and playing music, and doing the many kinds of handwork I enjoy.

21

This is my story, at least up until the present. There will undoubtedly be more adventures ahead. My plan is to stay here in San Juan for the rest of my life. In a sense, there is no choice, since I could not afford to live in the U.S. anymore and would be unhappy living in the type of country that it has become. I also would be hard pressed to decide where I would want to go. All of my children have offered their homes to me, but even though the Nicaraguans manage with several generations living together, in our culture it seems more difficult. I think neither my kids nor I would be content with that arrangement for long. We have lived apart too long.

As I contemplate the future and my physical (hopefully not mental) abilities diminishing, I could not be in a better place than San Juan. The people here are very solicitous of older people and you feel their respect and caring. I would have no trouble finding someone to help me, even live with me if it was necessary, and I could easily afford their services. I would be able to stay in my own home with no trouble, thanks to George, who helped me prepare for the possibility of no longer being able to handle the stairs. It also helps keep me young to live among people who for the most part are younger than I. There are times when I long for the companionship of my contemporaries, particularly with Maggie no longer here, but I am at the age when my old friends are beginning to die, or are no longer able to travel. It's a situation we all experience eventually.

Never fear that what you give, either financially or otherwise, is too little to make a difference. I can attest to the fact that this small project in this small town HAS made a difference in many lives and repays me ten-fold for anything I have given.

I hope I have painted a picture of my life here in Nicaragua that stimulates your spirit of adventure to try new places and new things regardless of your age. I wouldn't have missed this experience for anything.

ACNOWLEDGEMENTS

To my daughter, Katie for her many skills: editing the manuscript, offering support and suggestions, doing the layout, and providing the title.

To my friend and former partner, Chris Berry, who shared my goals of providing jobs and education for the young people of San Juan and helped me attain them.

To Dan Polley and Cesar Paniamogen for their friendship and many contributions to the Foundation including their beautiful photos highlighting the beauty of Nicaragua and the vitality of its people

To my children who supported me from the start in what must have seemed like a drastic and risky move at my age.

To Sandra George, John Detwyler, and Arthur Hancock for their careful reading of the manuscript and for providing many helpful suggestions.

And last but not least to the people of San Juan who welcomed me into their lives and their hearts.